David Otis Mears

Inspired through Suffering

David Otis Mears

Inspired through Suffering

ISBN/EAN: 9783744758772

Printed in Europe, USA, Canada, Australia, Japan

Cover: Foto ©ninafisch / pixelio.de

More available books at **www.hansebooks.com**

INSPIRED THROUGH SUFFERING

BY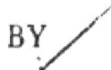

REV. DAVID O. MEARS, D.D.

*Author of "Life of Edw. N. Kirk, D. D.," "The Deathless Book,"
"Oberlin Lectures," etc.*

FLEMING H. REVELL COMPANY
NEW YORK   CHICAGO   TORONTO
Publishers of Evangelical Literature

PREFATORY

THIS volume is an essay to indicate the value of courage in the hard paths of life. A great deal that goes by the name of comfort is mere sentiment.

We have not limited the realm of sorrow to the death-chamber; living sorrows are sometimes, perhaps always, hardest to bear. Bitter anguish cuts into manly hearts in every-day life. Hard times crowd upon the most deserving. Deep anxiety plows its furrows in homes unmarked by crape. Hardships and sorrows are as varied as human experiences.

Comfort is as much demanded in the battle of life as in the loneliness following the finish of the fight. We need comfort almost more when hope alternates with fear than when the object of hope is gone; in the sick-chamber more than in the lonely room. The thoughts of these chapters take in the strong and the weak, the well and the sick, the struggling and the desolate.

An ounce of comfort is worth tons of pity. Pity discourages; comfort strengthens. Pity keeps hands off; comfort lifts up the trembling. Pity plays upon the feelings; comfort gives impulse to the strength. Pity repels; comfort wins.

A central thought concerns the greatness of human nature enduring or patiently bearing hardships. Strength needs the testing-time to declare it. Elijah was never commissioned to sit under a juniper-tree and moan. Christ fainted under his cross, but was never faint in courage. In like manner it is not manly to give up the battle when meeting some defeat. The immortal spirit of man was never made to fret itself away under adversity. It was a poor prayer of Elijah, "Take away my life." God has made us to rise above troubles; to make each one of these a stepping-stone to higher service. The lessons we learn make us stronger to help others. Sad experiences are severe teachers.

That life only is worth living that is lived for others. What we suffer is no excuse for closing our eyes against others' sufferings. Because we are driven to a lonely experience we are not therefore to keep away from those who are lonely. Because death comes to any home it is not that its occupants shall be dead to others' needs. We learn, to teach. We get wisdom, to give. We find paths, to show to others. We are fashioned through sorrows and hardships and difficulties, to be wiser, stronger, and better neighbors and friends. We are inspired to inspire. Our sufferings are teachers as truly as the inspired Scriptures.

God designs our troubles to make us larger and stronger. Christ was perfected through sufferings. Sufferers of the centuries have clung to him because of his being " touched with the feeling of our infirmities." What he was we in a measure must be: accessible to those who need our help.

If these pages shall inspire the troubled and bereaved and struggling to larger purposes, the writer's aim will have been reached.

CLEVELAND, OHIO,
  September, 1895.

CONTENTS

		PAGE
I.	Greater than our Burdens	11
II.	The Immortal Life	35
III.	Spiritual Helps in Earthly Hindrances	55
IV.	Patience	77
V.	Sympathy	95
VI.	Comfort	115
VII.	Inspired to Inspire	137

I

GREATER THAN OUR BURDENS

II

Man the personation of power.—Natural obstacles overcome.—Moral also.—Life, "labor and sorrow."—Moses' experience: he "endured."—Paul's testimony: "tribulations."—What his life-work cost him.—"Weariness and painfulness."—These men not pessimists.—These distinguished men examples.

Man stronger than his environment.—Burdens cannot crush.—Argument of Book of Job.—God has given us courage.—Life greater than its losses.—"Endurance" a quality of character.—We endure hard and disagreeable things, not the pleasant.

Test of human strength seen in what it can endure.—Adversity, test of life.—Financial panic tests the merchant.—Christ's seeming defeat a conquest.—Man preëminent over his conditions.

Surroundings no test of judgment; John Brown, Huss, Savonarola, Stephen, Paul.—Grandeur of human power.

Hardships and sorrows not removed by "endurance."—No two sorrows alike.—Each sorrow an individual burden.—Earthly limitations revealing human power.—Examples.—Hope depends upon what is unseen; Moses, Jenny Lind.—Man made to live even without sympathy.—Can "submit" and live.

Endurance of burdens a product of something higher.—Seeing the invisible.—Hope inspires "endurance."—Its deeds.—Things "not seen," the eternal.—The "image of God."

I

GREATER THAN OUR BURDENS

MAN is the personation of power. The scriptural record marks his preëminence: to subdue the earth and have dominion over every living thing. Even death is not defeat; man is immortal.

Human history records this power and dominion. Man builds roads over the Alps, and tunnels mountains for convenience. He spans broad rivers with cobwebs of steel, over which pass heaviest-loaded trains. He makes oceans his highways. He strings networks of wires over continents that shall communicate his wishes. He cables ocean-beds for use. He utilizes Niagara for power; and with this power stores the lightnings of the clouds to drive his factories and to forge his machines. He makes clouds and rivers and mountains and oceans his servants.

Dominion like this is not gained without toil, weariness, and cost; but these do not harm. Shall weariness of other kinds bring defeat? Are there not other "costs" of success? Is not man made to bear burdens, not to be crushed by them?

Without attempting any analysis just here of the common burdens in life, we notice the general fact. We borrow the testimony of two men whose success is beyond question. History, sacred and secular, records their names with reverence. Each speaks of the costs of his life, and of what life is. The one stood at the twilight of modern history; the other in the dawning day of the Christian civilization.

The first witness, in the Ninetieth Psalm, characterizes life as "labor and sorrow." This was Moses, the greatest name of humankind. Revelation exalts his rank in the immortal life in the sublime reference, "the song of Moses and of the Lamb." No other life has equaled his.

Modern civilization finds its earliest exponent in his teachings. His fame dims that of Abraham. He was the founder of the peculiar nation that has had its hand upon all governments. Grotius, that prodigy of learning, attributes the laws of Attica to those of Moses. He is the predecessor of Blackstone. His wisdom infinitely exceeds that of Solon. He is the world's first historian. As emancipator, statesman, lawgiver, historian, Moses merits the declaration of Dean Milman: "The Hebrew lawgiver has exercised a more extensive and permanent influence over the destinies of mankind than any other individual in the annals of the world."

It was this preëminently successful character who wrote out of his own experience, and from observation, that human life, even under the most auspicious environment, is "labor and sorrow." The writer to the Hebrews makes one word describe him—he "endured."

Recall a few facts. He was born poor. His life was saved from murder by the stratagem of his mother. By a remarkable providence, when he stood heir to the throne of the Pharaohs, he abandoned all claim to the palace. He chose "to suffer affliction with the people of God." He rejected the ease and pleasures of royalty. He preferred "the reproach of Christ" to "the pleasures of Egypt." He bore the unending complaints and murmurings of the people in all his active career. Whether we look upon him at "the back side of the desert" for forty years, or follow him during the extended wanderings, the conclusion is the same: "labor and sorrow." Moses lost what the world prizes, and gained what it shuns. Is he a fair example among men?

The same experience was met by Paul. He did not really begin to live until he cast away what he had once prized. He became an outcast. His family deserted him; more easily could he have mourned their death. He lost his enviable popularity in the great church of his fathers. He described his life as a continuance of "perils." The recital baffles description. He was whipped five times with thongs swung by the hands of Jews; and the madness of the whipper's heart gave full strength to every blow. He was stoned once; and fanatical hatred made the bruises deep. Three classes of men did their best to kill him—robbers, his own countrymen, and heathen. His life in wilderness and city was imperiled. He knew what it meant to be hungry and cold. "Weariness and painfulness" were frequent burdens. Storms of the deep waters were no greater perils than false brethren. Paul names his pathway "tribulations."

Thus these two greatest men of Scripture fame designate life as "labor and sorrow" and "tribulations." Both were the furthest remove from being pessimists. They abounded in hope. They were never cast down. Paul said of his tribulations, "I glory in them." Moses once almost gave way under the desperate strain of his burdens, even praying that he might die. But the despondency was only for a moment; his magnificent earthly life was ended with a song of triumph under a seeming defeat. Burdens multiply according as the work becomes greater. President Lincoln, during the war, probably suffered more than any other hundred men. We are not, therefore, saying that all men will have the amount of sorrow and tribulation that Moses and Paul knew, since all have not their responsibilities. It is not the amount that demands attention, but the fact.

The principle toward which such examples point, and in which they are involved, is evident: *man is larger and stronger than his environment.* No burden was ever heavy enough to crush manhood out. No sorrow was ever greater than the heart can bear. God never made a coward, nor has he anywhere held up as a model a nature that would break under sorrow. The whole Book of Job centers around this single test: that no affliction or evil could crush him. Man is not a worm to be trodden down, but a child of God. He is made to have dominion, to put all things under his feet. The agonies of Gethsemane may fall with frightful weight, but they cannot crush him. The cross will hurt, but cannot harm.

God has fibered us with courage, not with cowardice. "Ye shall have tribulation," the Master said: "but be of good cheer." He reminded his disciples of what they should suffer, but told them that their sorrow should be turned into joy. Physical pain may become torture; but manhood does not die with the pain. Loss of earthly goods will produce regrets; but there is an existence that does not depend upon earthly sustenance. Loss of loved ones shrouds the house in darkness; but the real life does not depend upon the beating of the pulse. There are living griefs far heavier than death; these bring sadness, but they cannot kill. The seer of Patmos caught the vision of multitudes who had come " out of great tribulation," not of those crushed by their burdens. Multitudes had become martyrs rather than surrender truth. Courage is the watchword of God to men.

It is not the kind of hardship that demands the endurance. Lives of Moses and Paul and millions upon millions of others prove that endurance is a quality of character. Whatever Moses met he endured.

The word " endure " refers to what is hard and disliked. We may patiently and lovingly endure those who hate us; but we never speak of enduring those we love. Christ endured the cross; it was hard. The word means more than patience. We must endure what we shall never like. Sorrows cut deep and are never pleasant. Paul was never pleased with his thorn in the flesh, and it was never intended he should be. God has given us the capacity to endure what we cannot help. In this power man is a king.

Notice just at this point that the test of human strength is seen in what it can endure, not in what it avoids. A small sail-boat might possibly cross the Atlantic from New York to Liverpool, provided there were no gales nor storms. This would not make it valuable for a winter's voyage. The strength of the suspension-bridge is measured by its weakest arch. The strength of the chain is just equal to its weakest link.

In a sense this is true of human life. One may pass easily along when things are smooth; yet the real test of strength is in hard times. All success depends upon endurance of hardships, not upon avoiding them. The sharper the financial panic the keener the test of the merchant's ability. The heavier the sorrow the severer the trial of manhood. Yet multitudes endure such a test. The world admires the heroism displayed in such a conflict. Men ask of one in financial trouble, " Will he succeed?" The inquiry concerning those passing through heavy affliction is, "How do they bear it?" Harder yet the living sorrow, that neither wealth nor position can assuage; yet all admit the heroism of those enduring it.

This is the severe way of reasoning to those whose hearts are breaking; yet it recognizes the preëminence of man over his conditions. In a sense this is conquest. There were prophecy, admonition, and assurance in the words of Christ: "In the world ye shall have tribulation: but be of good cheer; I have overcome the world." When he spoke the tramping of the soldiers under the leadership of Judas was already begun. The swaying of the lanterns and torches was in the direction of Gethsemane, whither Jesus was accustomed to resort. While the moonbeams lighted up with glory the trees of Olivet, the darkness around him was to cover agony itself.

It was in such an hour, under such conditions, the Master said, "I have conquered the world." Was this conquering—to be betrayed; to be forsaken by the Twelve; to be put to death? Was it conquering—to pass into Gethsemane, and to faint under the compelled burden of carrying his own cross up Calvary? The seeming paradox was the truth. Judas would succeed in delivering him into the hands of his murderers; but the infamous traitor must confess, "I have shed innocent blood." Peter would deny him with oaths, but before the first gray light of the morning he would bitterly weep. Pilate would try to wash his hands of their stains, but in vain.

We cannot always judge of men by their surroundings. John Brown conquered, though he was hung on the gallows; appearances were against him, but he had won immortal fame. John Huss conquered, though his winding-sheet was the flames that ended his life. Savonarola conquered, though the last sounds driven into his hearing were the hisses and curses of men calling themselves priests of the most high God. Stephen conquered, though his fading sight was upon the frantic efforts of infuriated men to rid the earth of his presence. The step of Paul was that of a conqueror even when he was led outside the Ostian Gate. Men cannot kill the truth with axes, nor burn it to ashes and cinders. The truth cannot be destroyed by fagots, nor cut by steel that can be sharpened upon grindstones.

The endurance of hardships and sorrows does not take them away nor make them more easy to carry. The home of those who once lived in affluence may at last be one of poverty. The wealth once owned may have shifted into the hands of sharpers. Disease may have paralyzed those whose ambitions are high, and life thus have become a burden. Sufferings in the family may have darkened all earthly pleasures by anxiety over the patient loved one in the enforced seclusion. The nights may increase the weariness because of the remembrance of some wanderer gone out from the home. Or the crape may have been taken from the door, while the home that misses the voice whose daily words were richer than music may seem empty forever.

The complexion of trouble is as varied as the leaves. No two sorrows are ever alike. The peculiar character, the strength of the love, the relations between the once loved and now gone—all enter into the peculiarity of each sorrow or hardship. No one is permitted to say to another, "I have felt the very sorrow you are passing through." Sorrows are as varied as have been the faces of our beloved. Our little child differs from every other child. Our parents differ from the parents of others. No two companions in life are alike. Since this is evident the sorrow of each heart must be as different from that of others as the personality has been.

Each sorrow is thus an individual burden.

Its anguish marks the degree of the love. The endurance of the burden indicates the ability of man above his environment. We need sympathy; but even if sympathy were withheld, man can live without it. Friendship is a mighty help; but even though all friends should fail, man can struggle on alone. He is able to endure a thousand burdens that crowd upon him. He can endure crushing weights that ought to be spared him. He can submit—that hard word expressive of a severe experience—to what he cannot explain. Jesus of Nazareth trod the wine-press alone; in this he was a pattern for multitudes.

This grandeur of human power is manifest in the every-day success of men whom early deprivations schooled into self-reliance. Barrenest pastures and fields have seemed to turn out strongest men and women. Nearly all our most illustrious statesmen have grown strong through the limitations of poverty. It would be almost invidious to name them—Webster, Clay, Garfield, Lincoln, and hosts like them. Republics and lesser organizations do not place reliance upon any who are not self-reliant first; and self-reliance thrives best when others fail to help.

It was the prayer of Luther written into his "will": "I thank thee, O God, that thou hast made me a poor man on the earth." The great reformers have nearly all been children of poverty, whose sufferings could not crush them. Literature is a fruit of sufferings in countless instances. It seems strange that "Rasselas" was written to defray the funeral expenses of the famous writer's mother. During the time of Sir Isaac Newton's greatest discoveries his tax of two shillings a week to the Royal Society was a positive burden. Millions charmed by the "Wizard of the North" do not ponder the burdens of debt overcome by the work of his magic pen. While princes, bearing the name of rulers, have been whiling away their time upon trifles, many a subject has risen above and out of hardships into greater than kings. The most illustrious names in Westminster Abbey are not of those who have worn crowns.

The annals of the world's benefactors contain the names of those who have conquered sharpest difficulties and proved themselves greater than all their burdens. Whatever the condition or environment, man is superior to it.

Human endurance is largely a product of something above and beyond itself. Moses saw the throne of the Pharaohs, yet knew of another infinitely higher, and so refused the lower. He recognized the pleasures of sin, yet saw a far higher enjoyment in doing his duty—that word so often meaning drudgery and pain. He saw the riches of Egypt, yet looked upon rich treasures that Pharaohs never can handle or count. "He endured, as seeing Him who is invisible."

Modern life is not wholly barren of such sacrifice for principle. The biographer of Jenny Lind has pictured her sitting close by the surfs that were rolling in from the ocean. Upon her knee was a Lutheran Bible; while closing down upon the westward waters was a sunset of surpassing splendor and beauty.

The world had been entranced by this gentle woman, whose voice gave hints of what angels' voices may be. Crowded assemblies had called and recalled her again and again to look upon her face and hear such notes as other human lips have never rendered. The wealth of continents had striven to give its owners a place where the enchantress of song ruled. It was a friend who asked why it was she had abandoned the stage in her early career, when at the very height of the most brilliant successes. To the question the great artist quietly replied, "When every day it made me think less of this" (laying her finger on the Bible) "and nothing at all of that" (pointing to the sunset), "what else could I do?"

In that gentle answer breathes a principle no one can neglect. The most winsome, flattering enchantments of life must never be allowed to usurp the place God holds. The presence of the great singer had been sought by the royal houses of Europe; kings and queens had given her the homage of unsullied admiration; millions had crowded the halls where she sang; but whatever should draw her thoughts from God's Book, or turn her attention from the sunset splendors, must be surrendered.

There is a divine compensation for every true sacrifice. Why is it men can endure crushing burdens? How is it they can bear losses without flinching? Can there be endurance without hope? If there is no object ahead in life, can we endure the drudgery? Is there comfort to those who know no future life? Hope is an inspiration. It banishes fear. To lose hope would be to lose all.

The pathway of each life is strewn with broken plans and unfulfilled expectations; but the things now shattered inspired at first. We live in hope. It is the cheer underlying every great action. It is proven in every ship of commerce plowing the seas. It stimulates all courage in business. It quickens the deeds of the plowman, preparing his harvest. Hope never dies till the man dies. Yet even hope may be false. It may be bright in youth; in prosperity, when time flows smoothly; but if it fails in sickness, or loses its grip in discouraging times, its falseness is manifest. It has followed a rushlight, supposing it a beacon.

Endurance of burdens depends upon seeing the unseen. When wealth is swept away, seeing Him who is invisible means seeing greater riches and treasures than gold. When earthly honors are lost, seeing the invisible means looking upon the higher throne of power. When grief rolls in its floods of agony, seeing the invisible keeps our thoughts above the terrible darkness. The rainbow is brightest on the blackest cloud; so the strongest hope and courage may rest over hearts that are plowed by heaviest griefs.

Seeing Him who is invisible means that this life is not ended by death. No more hunger; no more pain. All tears shall be wiped away. No more need of sunlight; God is the sun.

The best part of the true life comes after this life is finished. The things that are seen are temporal; those not seen are eternal. The revelations of Scripture agree with man's own nature; he is larger than his troubles, superior to his environment. Made in the image of God, he can endure and work, endure and wait. He can bear labor and sorrow, and at last catch the vision of Beulah. He can say all through the pathway of labor and sorrow, "I have conquered." When he treads the last dark valley, it will be the assurance of conviction he speaks: "I have conquered the world." He can live without receiving pity. Though sympathy were denied him, yet the strength is in him. Man is greater than all he suffers; larger than his largest sorrows.

"How wonderful is man!
Connection exquisite of distant worlds!
Distinguished link in Being's endless chain!
Midway from nothing to the Deity!
A being ethereal, sullied, and absorbed!
Though sullied and dishonored, still divine!
Dim miniature of greatness absolute!
An heir of glory! a frail child of dust!
Helpless Immortal! Insect infinite!
A Worm! a God!"

II
THE IMMORTAL LIFE

Profit and loss of life real or fictitious.—If death ends all!—Immortality as a motive.

Two facts: our weakness and possibilities.—Tabernacles to be taken down.—Materialism borrows language of the spiritual.—Comparison between the temporal and lasting.—Mansions outlast the occupants.—Immortality in the human face.

Undying desire for undying life.—Death the history of the race.—Christ conquered death.—Immortality a human intuition.—This conviction gives power.

First: Every-day burdens.—Living troubles.—The immortal not dependent upon temporal things.—World powerless in making weak man strong or strong man weak.

Immortality makes great hope; develops abilities.—This intuition met by Christ's assurance.—Life of Jesus; Paul.—If life ends with the flesh, most helpful and wisest of the race have been deceived.

The immortal and earthly " goods."—Immortal man infinitely superior to all he can handle.

Secondly: The burden of grief.—The lonely home.—Stoicism hard; Jesus wept.—Christian to love; Christian to weep.—Life not ended here.—Hope, compensation for broken homes.—Love makes heavy burdens.—Max Müller quoted.

II

THE IMMORTAL LIFE

THE "profit and loss" of life is real or fictitious, according to our standard. If death ends all, life is all a loss. It would then endure its hardships, carry its burdens, and pass away with no satisfaction to itself. It would endure hard struggles in commercial or other directions, and die unsatisfied. It would deny itself for the children, only to leave them forever. It would stand by the bedside of the idolized child, and turn away from the beautiful though lifeless form without one ray of hope. If there were no continuation of life independent of this physical body, it would not be worth living.

The conviction of the immortal life changes our estimate of everything. It impels hope. The poor anticipate a balancing of seeming inequalities. Sufferers speak of a world where there is no pain; where they never say, " I am sick," where there is no hunger nor thirst. In such a hope and conviction the dying assure us we shall meet again. The added years do not bring dismay. The weary and the aged speak complacently of laying down their burdens for the burdenless existence.

Two great facts confront each one of us, our weakness and our possibilities. The one pertains to the body of flesh, the other to our spiritual nature. We dwell in this tent of the flesh. We have a body; it is our possession, not ourself. It is not the hand that thinks, nor the eye that plans, nor the face that loves; hand, heart, and face declare in a physical sense what the spiritual being within wills and controls.

Take human existence, called life: it begins

cramped by the weakness of infancy; it grows up under the bounding impulses of youth; it braves the burdens of what is called maturity; it seems to droop under the weariness of age; the steps become more slow, the frame begins to totter and tremble; slowly but surely the mortal powers give way, until the strength is all gone; yet through it all there has been but one life lived. No human eye has seen the life; no ear has heard it throb; no hand has touched its vibrations. The body drops through decay into the grave, but the life does not die. The spiritual nature or body occupies for a season the earthly, material body that is always dying. The Apostle reminds us that we are living in tabernacles that must be taken down; but the real life does not depend upon the tent.

There is not a materialist who will not, in his denial of the spiritual, say, "When I was a child," or "When I was a youth," or "When I became a man." Infidelity and materialism beg the very language of the spiritual in their self-assertions. The real nature, the immortal or spiritual, retains its perfect identity unchanged in an ever-changing body. In other words, the unseen in man, the ego, is himself. Individual human history is thus summed up: "I was born; I have spent my youth; I have passed through manhood; I am sick; I am dying." And yet with the man of great intellect, when death had clutched his vitals, every one can say, even in the last moment, "I still live." Dropping this body of flesh is not death; it is only the true and higher nature breaking away from that which was made to perish.

It is strange that so many forget the distinction between the temporal and the lasting. The houses we live in, the trees under whose shadows we rest from the heat of the sun, the gardens we plant, the orchards we cultivate, the highways we tread—everything upon which our vision rests is temporal and is passing away. Time never ceases carving its lines into granite and marble. It is relentless; it plants its mosses over names upon the tablets of the dead. It is a power, sweeping whole cities out of sight.

Still, the mansions outlast the occupants. The buildings survive the builders. Compared with the human frame, granite is almost eternal. Flesh is perishable as grass. The heart tires out before time has gnawed into the granite. The fleshly body is temporal, like the house under whose roof it rests, only far more frail. The body dies, but the man never. The mansion decays, but the occupant lives. Our real life is the immortal.

It was said of a distinguished scholar of this generation that no man could look into his face without believing in immortality. There is nothing so expressive as the human face. It may be a child's face; yet there are seen depths of eternity in the child's eyes. Man is more than a walking pillar of dust. There is an infinite pathos back of the human voice. Thought is at an infinite remove from the organs that give it utterance.

In this conviction of the dual nature of man the latest science and the Scriptures agree. Man is preëminently an immortal being dwelling for his earthly life in material form. We who briefly deal with material affairs are to live on when the last of earth has come.

Within every one dwells this undying desire for an undying life; but after the most has been said, the history of human life is equally the history of death. There has always been a shrinking from the great change. It has made the gloom of Egypt deeper; it has put out the light of Athens; it has darkened the snowy summit of Olympus; it has bated the breath of men professing no timidity. Men have feared the Hannibals of history, but they have feared death more. They have shivered within sound of Alva's sword, but have preferred a life amid cruelties rather than a silence in death. With all the strength of hope there lingers yet in every human breast a shrinking which the power of God alone can remedy.

Unless Christ had allayed this fear; unless he had revealed an immortal life transcending this, before whose splendor the brightness of this world is as a cloud; unless he could, and did, prove himself mightier than death, his mission would have been a comparative failure. He might have given sight to all the blind in that ophthalmic climate; have swept the hectic flush from every fevered face; have banished all leprosy from the paths he trod; he might have left neither lame nor halt within the walls of any town whose streets echoed his footsteps; and yet, if he had not conquered death—that greater than fever or deformity or leprosy—his mission would have gained no hold upon the race. Passing into the hour of the great change, he could well say, "It is finished." If he had never cast off his transfigured raiment for the "decease he should accomplish at Jerusalem," we would still have been shrouded in the terrible mystery which the great fact of the resurrection from his tomb has dispelled. Our life is *in* the temporary house, but not *of* it.

Every race, from the most rude to those most cultured, has intuitively believed in immortality. The Scriptures assume it from first to last. Experts in science accept the same fact. Man is an immortal, a citizen of another world than this.

We have previously observed man's ability to endure hardships and disappointments and sorrows; this conviction of his immortal nature gives yet greater power. We notice two particulars.

First, *the every-day burdens.* Just as over nature cyclones and fierce storms sweep their destructive paths, so is it in common life. Panics disturb the commercial centers. Unscrupulous men imperil the credit of the honorable and just. Knaves ply their trade. Vile characters plot to defame the pure. Trusted companions prove themselves enemies. Living troubles crowd into the home. Hardship falls where once was ease.

The full enumeration of human ills baffles recital. What shall the "man immortal" do with these? Shall he grow timid because men clinging to commercial prosperity are afraid? Shall he weaken his manhood because men who have abandoned their manhood trouble him? Shall he forget his immortal destiny and its rewards because knaves do not know they are brutish? Shall he quail if any look askance, when he knows his purity of motive and conduct? Shall he fear when the once trusted reveal their meanness? Shall he shrink from his accustomed duties because others, whom he loves, destroy for themselves their promising future?

Human strength does not grow from the soil where thistles grow, nor come down from clouds where lightnings play. The magnificent forces of the republic cannot make a weak man strong nor a strong man weak.

One man with God is a majority. It is so ordered in the nature of things that every one may keep the place for which his character fits him. What, therefore, does this immortal do amid the burdens surrounding him and impeding his path?

A great hope makes great deeds. Cramp life to its existence here, and human aspirations are all dwarfed. Given larger possibilities for this existence, there are corresponding abilities developed. Strike away hope, and death begins. Let the idea that this life is all obtain, and the crowding evils and cares will bring despair.

This assurance of an endless life is a characteristic belief of the largest benefactors of the race. Christ met this longing for a higher life by his words, "If it were not so, I would have told you." If there is no endless life, the words of Christ in his dying breath were those of delusion: "Father, into thy hands I commend my spirit." If there is no continuity of life, the life of Christ in its self-sacrifice was a tremendous mistake. If the teachings of Paul were, and are, false, his magnificent career was only that of a fool. If the life we live goes down with the flesh, the best men of the world have been deceived. In such a case Paul was courageous for nothing; martyrs and heroes were acting a foolish part. Does there not seem an incongruity in the idea of the wisest and most helpful of the race being those who have been the most deceived?

Our exalted conception of the immortal life makes even the legitimate affairs of this life seem tawdry and gross. How would an angel look counting money? We should doubt him as an angel. How would Gabriel appear giving his angelic attention to organizing a "trust"? The quaint dreamer pictures earthly things as refuse gathered with muckrakes. In themselves, all these are worthless beyond the limitations of earth. As inhabitants of the earth, however, we have to do with them. All are valuable in their place. Yet, if the loss comes, shall the immortal mourn? When bank-stocks grow less in value, shall this immortal imagine that God is leaving his throne? When knaves destroy his credit, shall he think that God's promise is failing? The wealth of a Rothschild is not of as much value to an immortal spirit as are our old broken playthings of childhood valuable to us. Who can imagine one of the redeemed sighing to come back to earth to take up a few mortgages? None could suggest any comparison between the mansion Christ has prepared and the mansion left behind on earth. We are to use these things as not abusing them; but we shall take none away with us. Why not, then, treat them at their worth, or worthlessness?

A kind word can do more for us than can the national treasury. The tear of sympathy is more resplendent of beauty than the most brilliant rainbow. "Crown me with flowers," said the dying Mirabeau; "I have within me a hundred years of life, but not a moment's courage." The courage he lacked was what the Christian faith would have given. When Collingwood, the old English admiral, was breathing his last, the captain expressed the fear that the tossing of the ship disturbed him. "No, Thomas," he replied, "I am now in that state in which nothing in this world can disturb me more." Immortal man need not wait till the dying-hour to learn of his infinite superiority to all he can look upon and handle. Immortals have to deal with perishable things, but we can live—at last we must live—without them.

Secondly, *the burden of grief.* Every home can appreciate the utter darkness possible even in the brightest day. Sunshine is sometimes almost a mockery. The music of birds, piercing the silent room, hurts. Voices of passers-by seem harsh. Traffic will not stop even if the crape is on the door. Twilight in its splendors brings imaginings of the city with its walls of precious stones. Creeping darkness makes a chill in the heat of summer. Glittering stars of night attract the aching hearts sighing for those who have taken the long, silent journey. Griefs come rolling over the heart as waves dash over the bather on the shore of the sea. It is terrible, this grief. No two days alike; listening always for the voice we cannot hear; speaking to ourselves the names of the loved and gone. Do they see us? Do they pity us? Will they not welcome us when we leave the earth? What rest in the thought that they know our unspoken sufferings!

This is the darker side. Stoicism does not weep; but Jesus wept. In the moment of the divine call Jesus knew his friend would come forth; but even he wept. Weep on, beloved. Mothers and fathers have wept upon the leaving of their children for school. Friends have parted at the wharf, their tears expressive of affection, even though expecting to meet again. We send after them our love-filled missives, whose writing is blurred with our tears. It is Christian to love; therefore it is Christian to weep. The enforced parting is hard to endure. The disappointment is bitter. We can never be as before. A part of our life seems gone. We find ourselves thinking when around us are busy tongues. We grow absent-minded. Grief is freaky and strange. But there is another side.

The conviction of immortality reminds us we shall meet again. We cannot sorrow as those who have no hope. Life is not ended with the last breath. The future claims the thoughts of the silent chamber. The immortal hope reaches forward. What else could give the needed consolation?

The home may have everything beautiful. Wealth may have lavished its luxuries upon each life; loving hearts have vied with one another in devotion. The almost idolized child is beyond the reach of highest medical skill. Her active mind has grown in power under most careful instruction. Her voice has charmed with its sweetest notes of song.

Music, as from harps of gold, has thrilled under her touch of the strings. Ornaments of her choice beautify each room in the home. She has been the companion of the mother, the comfort of the father. Her face has brightened the home, has given happiness to those she has met on the street. The poor have kissed her shadow in passing. The aged have wondered how she gave them such joy. Little children have flocked to her side for recognition. Can she be spared? A sweetness unearthly rests upon the beautiful face. Lingering love draws in closer embrace those who would gladly die for her. No tear on her cheek; she is going home. Hers is the only brave heart. Fond hopes of parents broken; cherished plans for life destroyed! Is this all of life? Can such as she die? Is that growing character and power to end? The world to come is larger than this. Its ministrations are ceaseless, its companionships eternal. Only immortal hope has power to give comfort in such surroundings, and to make the desolate calm. How else can the parents take up the heavy burdens connected with that sad home? Nothing but the assurance of "the better land" can solve the mystery of their bravery.

Many a home has been softened and blessed in the memory of its promising son, too early gone. Tears dim the eyes of the lonely parents, waiting to meet him again. Threads of silver are crowding in more quickly since the last good-by. The father had expected to lean upon him; but every nook and corner of the homestead are vocal of him they cannot see. The mother's heart was almost breaking when she kissed him the last time. The conversation constantly recalls his name, as the two, stricken with grief, muse alone the long winter evenings. Their boy is not dead, only gone before. They wonder if immortals change with the passing roll of existence. They question how he will appear when they shall meet him again. They wonder if the active spirit finds time to think of them. Dreamy questions crowd one upon another in quick succession, but all explain their conviction of his immortality. Love makes heavy burdens, burdens we would never forget. We cherish memories that bend us down; but our thoughts are strong in the immortal life.

"Without such a belief," remarks Max Müller, "religion surely is like an arch resting on one pillar, like a bridge ending in an abyss."

III

SPIRITUAL HELPS IN EARTHLY HINDRANCES

Daily perplexities and cares spiritually helpful.

Three sources of troubles.—From outside interference.—Blunders.—Innocent involved.

Troubles increase with our duties.—Thrift follows piety.—Most devout will have most care.

Our double service, to God and men.—Love met by jealous antagonisms.—Greatest troubles come to greatest helpers.

Troubles in proportion to affection.—Love produces anxiety.

The stronger the love the heavier the coming grief.—Burdens and hindrances a logical necessity of a loving, useful life.

Relation of hindrances and trials to the spiritual life.—Growth by overcoming.—Adversity a school.

Piety helped by common drudgery of life.—Best people the hardest worked.—Paul's tent-making.—Wilberforce.

Annoyances better borne than removed.—Washington. Waterloo the fruit of reverses.

The mission of pain and trouble.

Golden experiences grown in dark days.—Joseph; Bunyan; David.

God never unjust.—Reaping what we have sown.—Everyday things God's instruments.

Wellesley College, fruit of grief.—Life a battle.—Best lovers of their kind those who have lost most.

III

SPIRITUAL HELPS IN EARTHLY HINDRANCES

IT is one of the commonest mistakes to assume that our daily cares and perplexities hinder the growth of the spiritual life. The prayer is for prosperity, while adversity may have the best lessons to teach. Many assume that people are good in proportion as their cares and anxieties are less; while the truth often is these very cares and perplexities help them to nobler living. We turn our attention to this seeming paradox. The chiefest saints have often been the chiefest sufferers; is this the law?

Three sources of troubles demand recognition.

Troubles arise from outside interference. People are always blundering somewhere. The innocent are involved in the consequences of others' wrong-doings. Many have seen the savings of a lifetime swept away by some defaulter.

It is a sad story the world has to repeat. Careless deeds bring death to many a home. So-called circumstantial evidence has sometimes imprisoned the innocent. Things are not always as they seem. Places of infamy breed their destruction upon communities that beg in vain for their removal. Legislatures sometimes enact laws framed by lawbreakers, making immorality legal. Public opinion vacillates under strange leaders, whose vagaries mean unrest to the law-abiding.

Burdens multiply upon multitudes innocent of their cause. The inflictions are direct and indirect, but the fruits are often alike. Selfishness seeks a vantage-ground for its depredations. Sharpers rob the unsuspecting.

Children are not safe from human fiends. Young and old share in the results of outside annoyances. It is the consequence of sin.

Yet, aside from the environment others have made, we observe the burdens and hindrances incident to our own callings.

Troubles increase with our duties. It is just as necessary to be faithful in temporal as in spiritual things. It is just as much a Christian duty to be diligent in business as to be fervent in spirit. It may be truly affirmed that God abhors a lazy man. The best Christians are they who have the most to do every day. Faithfulness in the larger duties of the spiritual life will be manifest in faithfulness in the least things of every-day life. It is a fair question whether a mere tramp can be much of a Christian. Thrift follows piety. Awakening the mind to eternal things in their boundless grandeur compels more attention to the affairs of every-day life.

In other words, since the religious hope demands greater progress and attention in reference to earthly things, and since hindrances increase with the efforts required, our obligations to duty will doubtless increase the hindrances in the way of the most devoted Christian. They who attempt least will probably suffer least. Easy-going people make little effort and find few hindrances. The larger the business the heavier the difficulties to be overcome. The larger the ambition to do good the more the way will be hedged about. The more careful the housekeeper the more perplexities she will have. Troubles multiply according to the height of the ideal.

The most devout among men will therefore have more cares rather than less. Diligence in business requires the putting forth of greater efforts, and these efforts bring on greater solicitude.

Scriptural teaching requires of us a double service, love to God and to men. If we love

God we shall do our best for those about us. As spiritual beings we are compelled to live according to such a standard. This is no easy task. The living means doing and progressing. It means becoming better ourselves and making others better. It demands obedience to the moral rather than to the merely economical. It will probably clash against popular theories. It may cut down dividends as abolitionism did the profits of the mill-owners of New England. It may invoke the hatred of the rum-power when one tries to save the drunkard. It will exasperate the corrupter of morals when pernicious literature is destroyed.

The point we notice is: the higher the standard of living the heavier the hindrances. Corrupt men will fight against whatever touches their avarice or appetite. And yet more timid advisers may seek to intimidate also. The very line of every known duty leads through great obstacles.

History emphasizes such a fact in all its

chapters. Human envy and jealousy alone crucified Christ. James was beheaded to please the Jews, and for the same reason Peter was cast into prison. The Herods have been jealous of their thrones. Organized wickedness has always counted life cheap that has stood in its way. Upholders of human slavery inaugurated our civil rebellion. Ecclesiastical despotism kept up its Thirty Years' War. Reformers are always martyrs under hardships. Personal sacrifice is the price of doing good. In the line of such a certainty the great Teacher exclaimed: "Woe unto you, when all men shall speak well of you!" Such a "good feeling" would indicate that nothing was being done or attempted because there were no obstacles.

Troubles arise in proportion to the depth of our affection. The deeper our love the greater our anxiety for the object loved. They who have none to love have none to worry over. It is love that keeps the mother awake night after night, week after week, while the child is tossing with pain. Unnatural mothers give themselves no concern for their children. The degree of love measures out the mother's care.

Upon the same principle sorrows are proportioned to the degree of the love. We do not mourn for strangers whom we do not know. The stronger the love the heavier the grief that must some time come. Griefs, heavy and oppressive, result from a natural law.

In suggesting the sources of troubles we have not referred to seeming providences, with which man has nothing to do. Cyclones plow their destructive paths, and often life is sacrificed. Earthquakes tremble beneath dwellings whose occupants cannot escape. Lightnings strike from the skies where but an hour ago the sunshine gleamed. Volcanoes heave forth lava and ashes upon whole towns, burying them from the sight of the living. There is much that we cannot avoid; yet people move into earthquake countries, and take up reservations that are subject to deathly harm, and build close to the volcano's crater. A large number of the so-called providences are chiefly human risks knowingly taken. But concerning providences we do not discriminate.

In the order of nature burdens and hindrances are a necessity. Since the path of duty compels more burdens, and since love makes sorrows, it would seem that they must have some power upon the sufferers themselves.

What relation is there between the spiritual life and these inevitable hindrances and trials? The hindrances and burdens help rather than hinder. We grow by overcoming. Every difficulty overcome by the business man makes him stronger. There were seemingly insurmountable obstacles to the development of the steamship; yet these made Fulton stronger, as he conquered them one by one. Every assault against John Howard gave him stronger resolutions. The early hardships of Livingstone were an absolute necessity in the discipline fitting him for his magnificent work.

Business adversity does not produce prosperity, but it makes the courageous man strong enough to succeed when he tries again. Conditions and things are not separated into secular and spiritual, as regards their effects. Patience may be demanded alike by deprivation of churchly privileges or by an insect's sting. Under either contingency it is a Christian virtue to be patient. Christian endurance and resignation may be called for as much by what we personally cannot do as by what others may do.

Piety is not necessarily increased by avoiding the common drudgery of life. We could not become better Christians by going into the desert where there is nothing to be done. The very best people are they who are hardest worked in common affairs. Some one, meeting Wilberforce on the street, asked him, "Brother, how is it with your soul?"

"Really," replied the great philanthropist, "I have been so busy about these poor negroes I had forgotten that I had a soul." Can one doubt that such unconscious labors for those poor slaves made Wilberforce a larger and better man than could any amount of meditation? Paul's tent-making never hurt his piety.

The ten thousand annoyances and anxious cares are borne by those whose heavenly title is the clearest. There is an important discipline in these common things. Personal development under such is vastly better than the removal of them from our paths. The wearying cares of home may be brightening many a mother's crown of glory. The faithful man of business, in all his perplexities, can discern the perfect harmony and mutual helpfulness of every-day activities and spiritual growth in the apostolic injunction to be " diligent in business; fervent in spirit; serving the Lord."

Washington had more defeats than victories; but the defeats schooled the army into better discipline. Waterloo was the magnificent flower growing out of the soil of Wellington's many reverses. He is the best mariner who has met successfully the most gales and tempests, not the one who has kept by the wharf. All this is true in individual experience. The mistakes of the proud have often brought the perpetrator to the beauty of humility. Adversity has subdued rough natures into childlike sweetness. These annoyances are often the sharpest chisels in creating symmetry of character.

We could not be trustful unless compelled to look elsewhere for help. We should not learn patience unless severely tested in bearing burdens; thus the burdens are blessings in disguise. We should not be gentle unless we were first made to feel our own weakness. False friendships should make us know better the worth of real love.

We do not speak of small troubles; all

troubles are hard enough to bear at the best. A speck of dust in the eye can make misery. One little pain can cause a sleepless night. One harsh, thoughtless word can make another suffer days and weeks of torture. One expression of ingratitude causes a burden of crushing force.

Gentle, loving hearts often suffer most keenly when they do not understand how very beautiful those very sufferings are making their characters. Cripples who have never been moved from their chambers for a generation have among their number those whose faces are angelic. The greatest comforters of the poor are they who have met with greatest losses themselves, and who know the two extremes. The most welcome helpers in the chambers of sickness are they who have known best the meaning of pain. The truest comforters in homes of sorrow are they who have had the most of sorrow themselves, provided they have profited by the experience. Volumes might be written upon the mission of pain and trouble. Such biographies would touch every human life. Sometimes these hard experiences are needed to stir people up to a perception of what they ought to be and do. Even injustice may become a goad to the development of courage.

We must not be understood as saying that the benefit is in the pain or hindrance or sorrow. Such discipline is profitable only to those who try to learn the lessons. All the storms, mingled with the sunlight, cannot make flowers grow upon the Sahara. The mellowest sunshine and the gentlest rain upon the rock will leave it only a rock. To catch the meaning and value of these things our spiritual natures must devoutly meditate and pray for help.

Many people discount even the sunshine. There are those who are always cynical and sour. We must make every trouble helpful to ourselves, or it will make us morose and unapproachable. The hard things are calculated to make us grow better. In one sense they are as important in the development of our characters as is the revelation of God in Scripture. The Bible tells us how to grow; reminds us of the great principles underlying the successful life; gives the reasons for much we could not otherwise understand; but the things we daily meet are the practical tests found in our way. The earthly dark day ought to make a golden spiritual experience.

The brightest days have followed the blackest in history. Had Joseph not been sold as a slave and cast into prison, he would never have been the Bismarck of Egypt. Had Paul not been repeatedly dungeoned, he might not have found time to write the epistles that have inspired the centuries. Had Bunyan not been thrown into Bedford jail, the world would have forever missed his immortal "Pilgrim." The Psalms of David were written out of his sufferings. "The songs in the night" count up the longest list.

We are not inquiring into the origin of evil.

One fact is sure: God never has been cruel. He has never done an unjust thing. He has never needlessly caused a single tear. He has never inflicted one hardship upon even his weakest child. Scriptural philosophy teaches us that death has come by human sin. Divine laws have been interfered with. Man reaps the harvest of his own sowing. Heredity carries with it consequences of what others have done. This is the inevitable, inexorable law. The sufferings of Job are all under a divine permission, not creation. "God cannot be tempted with evil, neither tempteth he any man." Our thought is in the line of Paul's assertion: "We know that to them that love God all things work together for good." Burke truly spoke of "that great chain of causes which, linking one to another, even to the throne of God himself, can never be unraveled by any industry of ours."

These things "work together for good." All belong together, and each helps interpret the rest. Hammers and saws and planes are all necessary under the architect's supervision; but the great Architect uses every-day things for chisels and hammers and implements to smooth down the roughnesses that would otherwise be left in our nature.

It was a severe disappointment when a young man, because of impaired eyesight, felt impelled to give up the chosen profession of his life—the Christian ministry; but this disappointment gave him power in other directions. Williston Academy of learning bears his name, while many other institutions attest his munificence. His disappointment was for his personal good and a benefit to others.

The beautiful college on the banks of the Waban owes its foundation to sorrow. Death took from two loving hearts their idolized son. The desolation of that sumptuous home has ever since been changing multitudes of lives. The father found in that sorrow his abiding faith. He had been a leading member of the brilliant Suffolk bar; but he closed his law office. Heavy retainers had been his every-day possibilities; but these he took no longer. His equipment for life had been wholly in his profession; but he turned his face from all this. The sorrows through which he passed led him to plan for others' good. The pain he suffered led him to live for what he might give, not for what he might get. The father's and mother's sorrow gave the world its Wellesley College.

Sorrow in a palace made possible the further exploration of Africa, in order that its mysterious history should be brought into the light of men. The heart of the king was turned from the death-chamber of his beloved son to enfranchise the continent by opening its doors to the world.

We are not made to sit alone in sorrow or wilt under hardship or trial. The hard things, the hindrances, the trials, the obstacles, we must accept as a part of our schooling. Out from such a discipline we must come stronger and better. There is something magnificent in a manhood that will not flinch in adversity; that has a strength within mightier than all the forces of opposition without; that braves storms until the skies have become clear again. This is strength in exercise.

Add a few years and the fascination deepens. Time has made havoc with the smoothness of the face; the hair is white with glory; the slower step reminds of the weariness in walking rough places; the subdued voice echoes the attained wisdom. Like the ship that has breasted the wintry storms of the Atlantic, like the eagle that has winged his serenest, loftiest flight, like the cliff whose deep-seamed rifts declare what waves of wrath have dashed upon it in vain—such is life going out of this school of discipline into an existence where angels walk with the redeemed.

The losses of this life, the companions gone, the homes broken, the memories left—all these give a tenderer affection for the living. The best lovers of their kind are usually they who have lost the most.

> " Let us be patient; these severe afflictions
>   Not from the ground arise,
>   But oftentimes celestial benedictions
>   Assume this dark disguise.
>
> " We see but dimly through the mists and vapors;
>   Amid these earthly damps
>   What seem to us but sad, funereal tapers
>   May be heaven's distant lamps.
>
> " There is no death; what seems so is transition;
>   This life of mortal breath
>   Is but the suburb of the life elysian,
>   Whose portal we call death."

IV

PATIENCE

Ruskin's "rests" of life.—Patience hard to exercise.—Severer test than faith.—Endurance a necessity; patience a virtue.—Its character.—Illustrations.

Patience more than love.—Hardest lesson.—Does not blunt the sensibilities.

First, patience needed because of the unattained.—The ideal; sacrifices for reaching it.—Not natural to anticipate obstacles.—Life never as we plan it.—Patient or impatient under griefs.—Fascination in character softened by patience.—Hearts beautified by sorrow.—Patience winning others to itself.

Secondly, patience under discipline accords with purest reason.—Compels appreciation of endless life.—Impatience unreasonable and unmanly.

Thirdly, patience is the method of personal development.—God never frets.—Slow process of creation.—No haste in the divine plans.

Human perfection hard fruit to ripen.—Ideal always ahead of attainment.—Struggle is serious.—Thoughtless words; opportunities neglected; anger expressed.

Patience under our own weaknesses.—A noble life a slow growth.—Patience begins at home.—Fault-finders.—Patient heart serene under trials.—Provocations from without.

Patience means suffering.—If the occasion is removed no patience needed.—It keeps suffering.—Poor and rich need it.—It is heroism.—Its virtue shown from its opposite, impatience.

Religious hope better seen in patience than in love.—Differing temperaments.

IV

PATIENCE

IT is a beautiful thought of Ruskin that in the music of our lives God has inserted "rests." The imagery is of the chorus all silent, the artists waiting to sweep the strings again. The great audience is almost breathless until orchestra and chorus shall burst into the grand harmonies from which they have rested. There is no music in the "rest," but it helps the music.

Patience is that "rest." It is harder to time the "rest" than to follow the leader's baton in the music itself. It is natural to be doing, to be heard, to carry along the waiting ones who depend upon our deeds. To sit when we wish to move; to rest when our hearts throb to give help; to wait when so much needs doing—this is hard. Inspiration reminds us that the husbandman has long patience waiting for the harvest; shall we have less? He sees the vines put forth their tendrils and leaves. The harvest seems assured, but he must wait whether or not frosts shall come, or mildews blight. His faith sees the harvest, but he must patiently toil on. Patience is a greater test of character than mere faith.

We are made to endure hardships and sorrows; but patience is a virtue, while endurance is a necessity. Endurance pertains to our natural strength; but patience belongs to the moral. People may endure burdens impatiently; but there is no virtue in this. Patience means bearing human weaknesses with a loving heart. It involves gentleness. It bears wrongs with sweetness. It will neither fret nor complain. It is the only virtue that will carry out the good will of the heart. It is an ornament of character.

Patience is regnant when the merchant can look bankruptcy in the face and calmly bear the loss. It soothes a nature fretting under ill health, and gently accepts the disappointment in the failure to carry out carefully laid plans. It dwells in the home whose desolate rooms echo the voice now gone; looks out of windows where loved ones once looked; remembers with keenest love the blessings of the life now silent; yet waits to understand the reasons by and by. Pain gnaws upon the nerves, but patience rises above the pain.

Patience is more than love, since even mothers have sometimes been impatient. Most loving fathers have fretted when they should have soothed the childish hearts. Patience is the hardest lesson given in the school of life. It is not insensibility to things that hurt; it does not blunt the faculties; it feels injustice most keenly. It does not make the grief less, but bears the heavy burdens without complaint.

We notice in a practical way the need of patience:

First, *we need patience because of the unattained.* Human ambitions are almost as far-reaching as the imagination. Large plans are made to be completed. Splendid castles are planned far ahead. The ideal stimulates life. Men deny themselves luxuries for the present, anticipating them by and by. They sacrifice ease and comforts for that which they seek. They toil early and late. Society is in this feverish haste.

Calculations of obstacles to the plans are not magnified. We imagine the delights that will come to the loved ones when the good day comes. Yet how few carry out their cherished purposes without obstructions! Wealth has wings and sometimes flies away. The crape on the door signifies thwarted hopes. The full ideal is not attained. Life never comes out as we plan its paths. People everywhere are speaking of what might have been. They are telling where they made the miscalculation, or they remind of the griefs that blasted every ambition.

It requires patience to bear these obstructions and changes with composure. We may endure them; but are we patient? Do they make us grow morose and complaining? Or do they make us more serene? They ought to help us become more loving; do they? One of these two characters follows each grief and disappointment; which is it?

There is something fascinating in the successful business man's career, when prosperity increases and prospects brighten; yet there is greater fascination in one who has suffered earthly losses, but whose character is softened and subdued into the beauty of patience.

There is nowhere a scene more beautiful than the home bright with activities of life and love. Center of attraction for young and old, it stands a joy in the community. Parental love vies with that of the children to give one another joy. But somehow the most loving hearts may be beautified by sorrow. Did you ever notice the change upon the mother's face whose heart keeps close to the beautiful child gone before? Is there sculptor's chisel that can work such changes upon purest marble as sorrows can fashion upon the human face? Was there ever painter's brush that could bring such fascination into the face on the canvas as patience brings to the original? How quickly the timid and troubled find their way to such for advice and consolation! How lovingly the eyes of all follow their steps! The heart-broken linger at their hearthstone. The thoughtless ask the secret of their power. What inspiration is it holding such sway over all hearts? Is it their love, or their faith? Write the word large; there is love and faith back of it—*Patience.*

Secondly, *patience under discipline accords with purest reason.* We repeat the thought: man is greater than his burdens. As an immortal none of these things can move him. Patience rests upon faith in God. Faith never questions that God does all things well. That there are things we cannot yet understand all admit. But aside from events that come, our independence of them is evident.

Shall one give way to despair if riches take to themselves wings? Not even one speck of our gold-dust glitters on the eternal streets. With all the terrible depths of grief, shall the Christian complain when the immortal visions burst upon the beloved? Reason compels an appreciation of our endless life and hope, and commands us to trust in patience. Reason accords with Scripture in asserting the nobility of man. It is unreasonable to fret and complain. Such are not signs of greatness or of deeper love. Impatience is unreasonable and unmanly.

Thirdly, *patience is the method of personal development*. It is the divine method. God is never in a hurry and is never late. He never frets. The slow processes of creation baffle our conceptions. A single coal-seam six inches thick contains more vegetable matter than a thousand years could possibly grow. The coal period alone counts up among hundreds of thousands of years. Geological research through all the periods and ages is but an unfolding of the divine patience. The almighty God waits for islands to rise from the ocean whose builders are only insects. He has builded continents by adding the slow deposits of sand, grain by grain. The book of nature is a demonstration of the patience of God.

The lesser things of every-day life remind of the same fact. Men get nervous and wish everything done in a day; but God's day is sometimes a thousand years. It requires months for the Almighty to perfect the flower that we tread underfoot in our haste. It takes him a whole season to finish the golden fruit that we can waste in a moment's time. He puts a thousand years into the majestic growth of the oak that the woodman can spoil in an hour. Though nations are suffering with famine, the wheat-fields grow not one day earlier. Though the ripening of the fruit by a week's time would vastly increase its value, yet man must patiently wait God's slower way. The conditions of haste do not enter into the divine plans.

Human moral perfection is a more difficult fruit to raise than orchards produce from thriftiest trees. Patience is more beautiful than any lily that has ever sprung from the soil. So long as we know better than we do, we have not reached the highest state. The ideal is always ahead of the attainment. Goodness as a limit is infinite as God, and no one can fully attain that which will completely satisfy. No one has yet attained, nor is already perfect.

From this discrepancy between the ideal and the attained we can understand the daily tax upon patience. We know what we ought to be, but are still far short of the standard we have set. The struggle is serious. It requires a stern control for these imperious natures of ours to keep still. We know the sacredness of our neighbor's rights; his faults are not at the disposal of our tongue, nor is his sensitive spirit open to our shafts of wit; yet the thoughtless word slips off our tongue, and we are further from the ideal than ever. We firmly resolve to help those who are truly in need; the resolution agrees with the ideal; it is the expression of our higher nature; but somehow we neglect the opportunity, and the sufferers can lay their woes at our doors, and the distance between the ideal and the attained is great. Again, we resolve that anger shall be kept down; but in some passing moment the virtuous resolve is broken in stinging words that fly from our lips.

We need patience more because of our own weaknesses than because of the weaknesses and encroachments of others. A high and noble life is no growth of a day. Repentance from sin is only the first step at the beginning of a better life. Conversion of the motive is profoundly important; but the

Christian life is far more than mere conversion. We are converted to grow stronger and better. The deepest convictions of sin come to those who are the most pure. The clearer our apprehension of God's infinite patience the more ugly will our spirit of impatience appear. A frown seen upon our faces by an angel's vision must seem worse to him than would the breaking of the ten commandments seem to us; so far more keenly sensitive is his sinless nature above our own. The purest hope will not undo the necessity of this larger virtue, patience.

Patience, like charity, begins at home. If the person is undisturbed within he will be little moved by things outside. A cloud in the sky will float over two persons, the one finding fault, the other calm and thankful. The difference is in the men, not in the cloud. The summer's sun finds some complaining and others peaceful; the secret of difference is not in the sun. Outside provocations will likewise have little effect upon those who are right themselves. Unruffled dispositions are not easily disturbed by unkindness or assaults of others. There are many who have more to contend with in their own dispositions personally than with whole regiments of people outside. Patience is largely a personal matter.

Still there are provocations from without. There are severe and unlooked-for disappointments. There are sad partings. Our bearing under these will largely indicate how patient we are; and the degree of our patience will indicate how great or how little is our trust. Analyze this whole question, and the result will compel us to look in upon self at last.

When tempted to impatience, think how great is God's patience with us. Since he bears with us so kindly, it is but our duty to bear the same kindness toward others. How hard to carry this principle out!

Patience means suffering; this is its derivation from its Latin verb. The suffering continues all the while. If the occasion or cause is removed, there is no need of patience. Patience means suffering under what we are called to bear. It is much easier to have faith than patience; more natural to have hope than to suffer for such a hope.

We may apply this meaning to the home of sorrow. Patience remembers; feels the agony there is in the silent rooms; recalls the past. If the sorrow did not press heavily, there would be no call for suffering. Patience is suffering; it is the burden of aching hearts. It is not rebellious. It does not dull the aching grief. It suffers on, in loving confidence and trust. It never, never forgets. It keeps to itself night and day the name for which it suffers. It never forgets the beautiful life that has given a radiance to the home in which the sufferers remain.

The more common affairs of life also demand patience. The poor have need of it, to keep them from giving up in despair. The rich need it, to give courage against the thousand annoyances on every side. Those high in position need it, to hold them up against a surrender of their trusts in the line of duty. It is the assurance that success will come. There is a French proverb that says, "He who does not tire, tires adversity. All comes right to him who can wait." Patience is heroism.

It is sometimes worth while to take a view of a subject from its opposite side. Impatience is an argument in favor of the virtue it breaks. It bears the mark of unbelief and doubt. It indicates that there is no rest upon God. It reveals a weakness unworthy our nature. It is childish for men to fret and complain. It is pitiable to see those apparently strong lose the guidance of reason.

The power of religion is better seen through patience than through love. While saying this we do not forget the difference in the natures of men. There are those of phlegmatic temperaments who might almost go to sleep under severe annoyances; these are not models; they have little sensibility. The power of divine grace is not recognized between men so much as between the two conditions of the same man, that of unbelief and that of faith. More grace is demanded to keep one of quick and over-sanguine temperament quiet and patient than for another who has no specially impatient temperament to combat. What grace will make of the dissolute Bunyan or the blasphemous John Newton is the test; not at all is it the question whether it will make the two behave just alike. It takes divine grace, however, to keep the average man from fretting; but the fretting reveals the lack.

It is our lack of faith that would allow our burdens to gain the advantage over us. As children of God we must exercise our lives in patience, and thus declare our abiding trust in him.

V

SYMPATHY

Patience and sympathy compared.—Sympathy greater than pity.—Sympathy more than compassion.—The "prodigal son."

Sympathy and compassion illustrated by recent cholera scourge in Naples.—Desperation of the sufferers; hatred shown those free from the scourge.—Greek nobleman and King Humbert.

Great character gives sympathy.—Christ's path thronged with sufferers.—Parable of the good Samaritan; its characters.

Deepest wounds not bandaged.—Anger back of words and knives the same.—Jericho road girdles the globe; avenues cover it; mansions built over it.—Sufferers in luxurious surroundings.

Sympathy proportioned to degree of degradation.—Prosperity calls for congratulation; adversity for sympathy.—Cause of degradation no excuse for refusal to give sympathy.—Prisoners need it; the sick also.

Sympathy proportioned to the helplessness of its object.—Multitudes helpless.—No question as to gratitude in return.—Cowardice to shun the object of suffering.

Sympathy means restoration of the lost.—Declares the worth of its object.—"Image of God, not a worm."—Value depends upon environment.—Prodigal lost because away from his natural environment.—Not reasonable to make great exertions for worthless things.—Sacrifice for gold.—The divine Sacrifice declares human worth in God's sight.—Loss of jewel in watch destroys its usefulness; lost.—Drunkard father lost to his family.

Convict in woman's prison.—Living sympathy demanded.

V

SYMPATHY

THE fact of human suffering is woven into two common, plain words, "patience" and "sympathy." Had there been no torn and disturbed hearts the world would never have coined them. Patience denotes the bearing of personal sufferings; sympathy, bearing the sufferings of others. Burke defines sympathy as a sort of substitution. Patience means our own burdens; sympathy, suffering with others who are burdened.

Sympathy is far greater than pity. Pity conducts itself as superior to its object. Pity looks on and observes what it has never suffered; sympathy walks with the suffering.

Pity looks down; sympathy goes down. Pity can stand afar off; but sympathy stands by the side of its object. Pity may even have contempt for its object; but sympathy never.

Even compassion may carry with it a certain superiority over the object compassionated; yet compassion means a deep tenderness of feeling for another. Sympathy, however, is more than compassion. Compassion alone is not enough. In the masterly drawn picture of the prodigal son, the father is represented as "having compassion on him." But, with a rare touch of descriptive power, the father not only "saw his son" and "had compassion on him," but he "ran, and fell on his neck, and kissed him"; this is sympathy. It is not only a deep tenderness for others, but putting one's self into their position and circumstances. Sympathy allows no lines of separation between ourselves and those we would help; it illustrates a perfect equality of condition as regards the suffering.

The difference between compassion and sympathy has been illustrated in a recent terrible scourge of the cholera in Naples. The deathly plague was confined to the filthiest sections of the city. An English physician describes the resentment of the people toward those who would give them help. Among the would-be benefactors was a Greek nobleman whose generosity was equal to his great kindness of heart. Day by day this nobleman went himself from house to house distributing broths and luxuries and medicines for the sick. To overcome their strange resentment he was compelled to hire them to take what his pity and compassion had provided.

The resentment grew continually deeper until, angered because he was able to relieve their wants, they assaulted him, killed his horses, broke his carriage into pieces, and almost succeeded in taking his life. Out from that plague-stricken district rose the hoarse cries of desperate hatred toward those living in the better portions of the city. They actually planned to carry their dead inside the mansions of the rich, that they might laugh when the victims of the plague should be carried from the homes where plenty and health were abundant. They determined to sweep the city with the dreadful pestilence.

Officers of the government were stationed where the awful threats proceeded, but even the government came near failure. The mob were almost in possession of means and power to carry out these threatenings against the city, when King Humbert came down from Rome. The wretched people hated the rich in Naples; but the king was also rich. They begrudged the health of the nobles; but Humbert was in good health. They hated those higher in position; but here among them was the one highest of all. He may have had no kinder heart than many living on the hill of the city. Yet they ran to him with their sorrows; they stood with bowed heads when he entered their poverty-stricken dwellings; they hushed their own moanings in his presence.

The secret of the king's power is thus depicted by the physician whom we quote: " He came among them as one of themselves. He shared their dangers. He spent his days in their poor hovels. He spoke to them in their own Neapolitan patois. He nursed their sick. He held them in his arms when they were dying. He wept over them when they were dead. He was their brother in their sorrow, and they were ready to do his bidding like little children."

The Greek benefactor showed compassion and pity; the king had sympathy. The Greek kept himself somewhat apart from them, even in his bountiful kindness; but the king dwelt with them and was one of them. No reflection shall fall upon the generosity of the nobleman who suffered at their hands; but the perfect sympathy of Humbert conquered their bitter hatred and violence. Compassion and pity looked down from the heights of Naples; sympathy came down from the palace in Rome. Sympathy is a master in assuaging bitter anguish and calming fierce hearts. Mere pity degrades. Pity may do for brutes; but men need sympathy. This is godlike.

Irrespective of the varying conditions of life, that character is of greatest value that seeks to give rather than to receive sympathy. The great Teacher was "touched with the feeling of our infirmities." His whole example was that of one doing everything for others. Nothing moved him as did suffering. His path could be traced by the flocking together of the poor and halt and maimed and blind. Sympathy means an actual realization of the golden rule, doing unto others as we would that they should do unto us. It means the spirit of Sir Philip Sidney, passing to another the cup of cold water with his dying hand, and uttering his memorable words: "Thy necessity is yet greater than mine." The real sympathetic life will give, even though it may not receive.

No such exquisite and comprehensive picture of sympathy has ever been given as that drawn by the great Teacher in the parable of the good Samaritan. Its outlines cover both the giving and the receiving of help. It delineates in imperishable colors each disappointing character. There lies the helpless man, wounded and in pain. Its actors are men, and not dead Orientals. The passions of life breathe in the varying moods of its characters. It is a picture whose setting is the world and not the narrow Jericho road. It belongs to crowded highways everywhere as truly as upon that desolate path. It points out what so-called " good men " may not do in the line of duty, and what " bad men " may do. It reflects the results of suffering upon individual character.

We may almost listen to the footsteps of the coming travelers, as did the waiting sufferer. Perhaps the languid eyes saw that the man approaching in the distance was a priest. Hope dawned in the heavy heart. Fresh from sacrificial duties in the temple, the wounded man must have looked to him for help. But this "religious" man cast a glance upon the sufferer and then passed on; his retreating footsteps faded gradually away until nothing was heard but the sighing of the wind in the trees of palm, unless it were the sound of the sufferer's moans.

Soon another traveler approached; it was the Levite. His lips were accustomed to chant the holy psalms and anthems of the temple service. Assemblies had wept over the plaintiveness of his notes. His daily songs were of One who should heal the broken-hearted and relieve the distressed. Again there was hope for the wounded sufferer, who might rightly imagine that deliverance was at hand; but again the doom of disappointment. The telling words carry a freight of meaning in them: "He came and looked on him, and passed by on the other side." Are human hopes thus blasted? Are human hearts thus cold and unfeeling? Are the priests and Levites all dead?

Again the silence is broken, this time by the hurried, measured tread of a burdened beast. The rider is in haste. No hope here —the traveler is an enemy. The nations of the two have no dealings with each other. Poor neighbors! But the traveler stops his beast; dismounts at first sight of the wounded man; sets about caring for him; and hope that was banished returns. The last man from whom to expect hope is the first to give it. How many times the like has been repeated in human experience who can recount? Sympathy does not always come from those who have called themselves friends in the past. When the once prosperous meet adversity, havoc strikes away many a false friendship.

Deepest wounds are not those that bandages can cover. Broken hearts cause deeper sufferings than broken bones. Worse bruises are made by the thoughtless than ever robber's club has inflicted. A malicious word can cut deeper than any knife. It is not the implement that inflicts the suffering, but the motive behind it. Anger back of the word is as cruel as anger behind the knife. There is hardship enough in every life without adding to it; enough wounds without adding to their smarting pains.

It is strange how many towns there are on the Jericho road. It seems to girdle the globe. So many have been beaten, wounded, and robbed, so many indifferent to the sufferings of life, that one questions where the Jericho road is not. Its paths have been macadamized into beautiful streets and avenues; but underneath fine pavements it still remains. Cellars have been dug right over it; elegant mansions reared upon lasting foundations; richest rugs have been laid upon floors of exquisite finish; golden mirrors reflect the sumptuous furnishings of tapestries and silks. The sufferers may recline upon elegant couches, but the Jericho road is there nevertheless. Silken pillows cannot soothe the wounded any more than can the rough stones of the highway itself.

Builders of warehouses have blindly dug deep foundations without seeing how straight the same road runs beneath them. Counting-rooms have been finished in richest woods; huge safes have been rolled into their places; vaults for greater safety have been cemented into security just where the Jericho road has its bounds. The merchant in luxurious office, counting and sorting bonds of millions, may be only the sufferer of the Jericho road transferred from the outside into the room—a sufferer all the while. Wherever there is a sufferer there runs, close beneath, the Jericho road that Christ pictured for all coming centuries to behold.

The philosophy of sympathy rests upon certain great facts.

Sympathy is proportioned to the degree of

the degradation. It belongs to those in adversity. It is demanded in the line of suffering. It was when the multitudes were weary and faint that Christ had compassion on them. Prosperity calls for congratulation; adversity for sympathy.

We are never to inquire into the cause of the degradation before rendering the needed help. The criminal, for example, belongs rightly in the prison; yet his wilful acts do not excuse us from carrying out the teaching of the Master to visit him. Agony of disease follows the profligate; strongest opiates may scarcely deaden the horrid convulsions; it is the consequence of wilful guilt that knew no shame; yet the cause of the degradation does not excuse from the divine words that are to be spoken: "I was sick, and ye visited me not." Our college settlements in the heart of the slums are Christ-like. The prodigal's degradation only deepened the compassion and sympathy of the father.

Sympathy is proportioned to the helplessness

of its object. It is the divine rule to do for those who cannot recompense again. The most helpless being that comes into the world is the little child; and if for a single generation all motherly sympathy should be suppressed, there would no longer be an immortal being on the globe. But there is other helplessness than infantile weakness. People large in stature may be just as dependent as the little child. Many a strong man has stood dazed and bewildered. Each life has had its seasons when it knew not which way to turn.

We are to be feet for the lame, speech for the dumb, hands for the maimed. We are never to ask whether the recipient will be grateful. Better yet that our left hand know not toward whom our right hand was stretched. We may not always inquire just how much of the suffering has come from negligence or lack of thrift. Real suffering, according to its depth, merits sympathy in return. The object by the Jericho road must be cared for according to our ability. It is treachery to duty to leave such care to others. It is cowardice to shun the path that robbers of happiness frequent, lest we may be called upon to deny ourselves for their sake.

Sympathy means the restoration of the lost. Its positive side is in the good it does because of the worth of its object. There is an old adage that man is a worm; but the "image of God" is not a worm. The coin that is lying lost in the desert is worth no more than the worthless sands on which it shines. Its value depends upon its environment. The sheep on the mountain has no more commercial value than the scanty, worthless mosses on which he feeds. The prodigal, cast out and despised, is worse than useless; he is a curse to the community; his pitiable condition, eating husks, makes even heathen despise him; but the real worth of the man depends upon getting home again as a dutiful son.

It is not reasonable to make great exertions for worthless things. Men have rushed across the continent to dig gold; but they would not go across the street to dig sand, if there were no value in it. Thousands upon thousands have left home and its comforts to brave the perils of frontier life in order to gather in diamond-fields the shining brilliants. It is the object of value that compels the exertion.

The whole drift of Scripture leads us to see how God has respected the splendid worth of man, provided he can be brought into the environment for which he is fitted. The gospel of Christ must be declared in all the world, wherever there can be found a single creature. The immense duty indicates human worth. No such message would be sent to mere worms. The gospel is the expression of the divine sympathy. The greater the degree of the expression the larger is the value indicated in the one sought.

The watch in our pocket may lose its use

simply from the displacement of a single jewel. So far as indicating the hour of the day, it may as well be a stone on the highway. The drunkard has befogged and dulled his reason; the man is lost. He ought to care for his children; but they have lost their father. He ought to advance the interests of the community; but he hinders them; he is a lost citizen. Until the jewel is replaced in the watch it is useless. Until the drunkard is restored to his right mind he has not the value to his home even of a dog to watch it.

Sympathy sees multitudes bewildered and lost; hears the moans of those who are not what they might have been in life; and then seeks their uplifting. It is a positive virtue that each one must exercise.

Upon the wall of a woman's prison hangs a picture of Christ before the woman who was convicted of her deep guilt. Against her traces of sin the face of the Master manifests its dignity and love. He is represented as giving her a new hope. Under the picture are the memorable words, "Go, and sin no more." Some years ago one of the most intractable of the prisoners was seen to remain at the close of the prayer-service. It was the suspicion of the matron as she watched the hardened face that some new trouble was brewing. Upon asking her reason for remaining alone, the guilty, degraded woman made the strange request that she might be put in the solitary cell. The uplifted eyes of the culprit were still upon the picture. The matron reminded her that she had but just come from a week's confinement in the desolate cell. "I want to go and be alone," said the woman, "where I can think about Him that is in the picture." For a week she was permitted to carry out her resolute desire, when she came out from the solitude to serve the rest of her sentence. The old look of hatred was gone; her deportment was above all criticism. She served her sentence and left the prison, living ever after an upright and pure life.

True sympathy in the heart will manifest itself outwardly. There is a gospel in the human face when the gospel is back of it. That living power should be mightier than painter's skill in depiction. Greater than such skill on canvas should be the transforming power in us to inspire those who have lost faith in the reality of a holy life. Sympathy in action has a mightier power than highest art can gain or can paint on canvas. We must be living witnesses of this living power.

VI

COMFORT

Comfort more than compassion and sympathy.—Courage more important than pity.—Physician between courage and pity.—Business troubles.—Comfort means giving strength to the man, not relieving him of his burdens.—Comfort is a power given one under adversity.—Greatness, not in avoiding hardships, but in bearing them.—Illustrated by Felicitas and her seven sons.

God our Comforter, Inspirer.—Severity of disciples' lives pointed out by Christ; needed no pity, but strength.—God did not take away one of their hard duties.—Comfort is courage to face the storm.—Value of this life in the good it does.—Savonarola and Luther in heavy labors.

Human comforters.—Paul's teaching.—Edifying men.—Strengthening needed from infancy to old age.—Webster and Napoleon ridiculed.—Great natures help.

Small men can destroy work of great artisans.—The young need strengthening or comfort.

God comforts that we may comfort others.—Paul's experience.—The beautiful seen in what has been accomplished through storms.—One who cannot stand without receiving comfort cannot give it.

Universal need of receiving comfort.—Suffering universal.—Strongest men will grow infirm.—Every hero in the "roll-call of faith" needed strengthening.—Grisi and Jenny Lind.

Comfort in making the anchor of the ship; made for use.

VI

COMFORT

ALL men seek comfort. The word means far more than compassion or pity. Pity tends to discourage; comfort to strengthen. Compassion leads to sympathy; but even sympathy may depress.

Pity given the sufferer would inspire no hope. Courage is a thousand times more important than the kindest commiseration in all conditions. Let the time come when business is slow; creditors are pushing hard; every energy is taxed to tide over the emergency; it is a hard struggle. What, at such a time, would be the effect of expressing pity? It would indicate the impression of distrust on the other's part. Rather, at such a time, a word of courage is worth a volume of sentiment.

Comfort means "to strengthen." The physician who should merely pity his patient would kill him. Disease may leave but one hope in a hundred for life. Shall the physician give ninety-nine hundredths in pity and one stray hope of comfort? The skilful expert fastens the sufferer's attention upon that one trembling chance; he drives back every thought possible in the ninety-nine adverse conditions; he sheds no tear of sympathy, and will keep from the room those who should thus despair. The strengthened courage in that one hope has saved many a life.

The man of business feels the pressure of nervous creditors. It is not the time yet to realize the value of his assets. A few thousands would save him his credit and carry him safely over. His books show a credit of half a million; but he is a victim of the times. He needs not the pity of other men who have failed under like circumstances; he means to keep his credit and his business. Let there come to him in this pinch one who has successfully endured just such a strain, and one ounce of courage would be worth a thousand tons of pity.

This is the meaning of comfort. It puts strength into one who is struggling on in the line of his duty. The business man might wish his neighbor would advance the small amount that would give relief in tiding him over; yet a word that would give him strength to do for himself would be of greater value than thousands of dollars. Comfort means giving strength to the man, rather than giving that which would save him the exercise of his strength.

The Apostle does not teach that God gives comfort by removing the stake in the flesh, but by giving help to bear its sting. It is not his method to give comfort by removing trials, but by giving strength to bear them. It may mean the parent watching over the weak and suffering child. All the world's brightness may seem centered in that one life. Giving comfort may not mean the restoration of the sufferer to health, but a divinely imparted power to be a hero under the terrible strain of anguish. Paul's comfort did not consist in avoiding hardships, but in overcoming them. The word does not mean "to soothe" or "console." It has in it the inspiration of a bugle summoning to rise above the conflict. It spurs on to death, if necessary, in the line of duty.

Early Christian history records the scene in which a wealthy widowed mother, Felicitas, and her seven sons were summoned before Publius, and were commanded, under penalty of death, to renounce the name of Christ. Her eldest son was whipped with thongs until life was nearly gone. "Renounce the name and live," said the officer, when the aged mother bade her son stand fast and live in glory. Under the furious blows of the whip he sank into death. In her tortured presence her next two sons were beaten with clubs, while her voice bade them remember Him who died for them rather than yield to brutish command. The fourth was taken from her embrace and flung from the rock near which they stood. The other three, one by one, were beheaded, while to each her words of courage were true to her faith. This was more than courage; it was comfort. It was a strengthening for duty; urging a heroism she herself at last exemplified in bearing her own torture until her head fell under the blow of the knife.

Comfort holds up the feeble hands, and boldly faces even hardships and death. Some of the world's greatest sufferers have a comfort that keeps them strong in spite of the staggering blows that have befallen them.

This word expresses more than mere human deeds. It draws its meaning from God himself, as the Comforter. Paul declares that the comfort of God is given " that we may be able to comfort them that are in any affliction." We are to give the comfort that we get. We are to strengthen others as we have been strengthened. There is divinity in the meaning of this word.

In order to a truer conception of the virility in this duty, we observe not only our relations to God, but also to one another. Our duty and its meaning are covered and explained in the message of Christ to his disciples. The whole address was a superb inspiration. They should not be comfortless as orphans; nor should they be left alone. More stirring words were never spoken; and never were men in deeper darkness or in sorer need. What Christ meant in the term we must accept.

Notice the application of the address and the event to human necessities:

First, *the divine Comforter.* This was the description of the Holy Ghost; not a mere consoler of homesick men, but an inspirer of their great work. Christ held before his disciples the severity of their mission. They were to be dragged before magistrates; they were to suffer persecution; the world that crucified him was to put them to death. Such was the forecast; but they were promised the Comforter. Did they need pity because of sufferings? They never asked it, and Christ never pitied them. They knew that the promised success of the new faith would madden the great church whose high priest had sanctioned the murder of Christ. It would be dangerous to preach the words he bade them preach. The advent of a Saul of Tarsus, imprisoning and killing the innocent, could be only a natural result of the new gospel they should declare.

Hence they needed comfort from the Comforter. His office-work was not to take away the severe duties, not to excuse them from proclaiming a single doctrine, but to strengthen them in these hard things. Comfort did not mean singing them to sleep, but inspiring them to grander exertions in the mighty work of turning the world upside down. The comfort of God means the courage to face the storm; never to flinch even in the presence of Herod or Agrippa.

The value of this life does not consist in the ease in which it is carried through, but in the amount of good it does. The labors of a Savonarola are herculean, requiring not pity, but strength from God; but his work must be done. The work of a Luther is imperative; the overthrow of superstition demands such a giant; but in the gigantic work the battle-hymn of the fatherland was the indication of the source of Luther's power: "God is our Refuge and Strength." This was but another way of expressing what Paul said: "I can do all things through Christ which strengtheneth me."

Secondly, *human comforters*. This is Paul's conviction as to the duty of all: "That we may be able to comfort them that are in any affliction, through the comfort wherewith we ourselves are comforted of God." In a word, as God strengthens us, we must strengthen one another. Our highest duty is not to have pity, nor to exercise compassion, but to give strength. Paul seemed to look upon every one he met as needing to be builded up. Notice how often he speaks of edifying men. For such a work he adapted himself to every one. This is the scriptural method. You cannot build men up by the mass, but one by one. This is accomplished only by adding to their strength.

This is the only kind of life worth living. There is nothing more debasing than its opposite. There are those who make sport of the ways of little children, raising a laugh at their expense. Is that adding strength to the little ones? Youth struggles upward through an awkward age; habits may not seem cultured; movements may sometimes be ungainly; thoughts may lack finish in expression; diffidence may obscure the real metal of character within. Youth needs encouragement and strengthening in its purpose; yet there are multitudes who give no help. They criticize where they ought to help; they laugh where they should encourage; they cry down where they should lift up. Townsmen used to joke over Webster's ungainliness; but in the passing of a few years, when the farmers of Salisbury were still hoeing weeds, the young man against whom they had raised a laugh was holding a nation enchanted with the display of his magnificent powers, cultivated in spite of them. The aristocrats of his neighborhood cast ridicule upon Napoleon in his youth because of the plainness of his dress and his poverty; yet, acting upon his maxim, "A career open to talent," he outweighed in his person all the rest of France in its most critical hour. The world at last gives honor only to those who have inspiringly helped others. No one of great nature ridicules the weak or undeveloped. Paul saw uncouth natures rising out from heathenism and recognized his duty to help them to the highest usefulness. Is our duty less?

A hod-carrier can deface a statue it has

taken a Michael Angelo to create. Vandals have destroyed some of the finest specimens of art the world has ever known. There is not a successful man of prominence to-day who has not achieved his success in spite of those who would pull him down. In mercantile, professional, and literary life the rule has obtained. Small natures try to hurt others; great, noble natures try to build others up. It required the heroism of Nehemiah to build the walls of the city of his fathers; but while he was building Sanballat became infamous in his meanness, trying to keep the walls from being finished. No patriotism, no grandeur of life and purpose, in Nehemiah's mean critic!

Look upon our young people in their endeavors to fit themselves for a larger usefulness; every one ought to receive help from each of us. There is not one doing a commendable work but needs the loyal help of all who love our Lord and Master. There is not one struggling to become better who does not need our encouragement; never our neglect.

While giving comfort is our duty, it nevertheless remains true that the duty is not always done. Paul says that God gives us this comfort that we may give comfort to others. God strengthens us that we may give strength. He inspires us that we may inspire. Everything is done through the comfort wherewith we ourselves are comforted of God. The greatest characters of the race seem to have missed this human help. Aaron and Hur did once hold up Moses' hands; but how many times they left him alone! In time of Paul's deepest need he experienced what he afterward wrote down: "No man stood with me." One may need that on which he does not depend. Some of the world's greatest benefactors have died, as did Beethoven, with the question on their lips, "Have I not some talent after all?" The ruggedest tree of the forest is that which the tempests of a thousand years cannot break.

The most beautiful ship of the ocean is not the one of freshest paint, or whitest sails, or heaviest anchor that has never fluked the ocean's bed; but rather it is that monster, resting at the end of the stormy voyage, whose paint has been scraped by the ice it has tossed back; whose sails have been stretched and blackened by tempests; whose decks have been swept by the hurricane that could not engulf its freight of a thousand souls; whose anchor bears signs of the immense grip it held against hurricane and angry seas, below where deep-sea fishes swim. Every one, like that ship, is measured by what he endures alone. The agonies of Gethsemane were met by the divinely given strength; but even more than in this angelic ministry the divine character breathes in those utterly desolate words: "My God, my God, why hast thou forsaken me?" No one can give comfort who cannot stand without it, if necessary. Though all men forsook Paul, the Lord stood with him.

Thirdly, *the universal need of comfort.* Even Christ needed the companionship of the three disciples in Gethsemane, and needed the strength the angel gave. In a higher sense, however, we need comfort as a giving of strength. The saddest phase of personal biography is that written by the wisest king. No one is strong enough to tread the earth alone. The comfort of God does not release from the necessity for us to give comfort. From the nature of man suffering is universal. No home escapes it, and no one. It may not fall upon all alike at the same time, but the haughty spirit will some time bend, the loving heart will almost break, the strongest men will grow infirm. Such is the sad, the universal law. Some one may suffer to-day, but somebody's turn will come next. The comfort we give to-day we may crave for ourselves to-morrow. There is not a hero in all the "roll-call of faith" but needed strengthening. The life of all is some time darkened. A tear is expression of heavy, bitter grief;

but tears are too many to be counted. Struggles are the order of the day; no one succeeds who does not struggle; and those struggling need strengthening. Suffering everywhere. Troubles crowd the joys. Each household in its turn is touched. The strongest men wend their ways lonely and bereaved.

Great need is there that out from all these troubles and all this darkness One should speak: "I am the God of all comfort." See what the Comforter made of the disciples, turning their cowardice into boldness without a discount. See the cringing Peter, afraid of the laughter of the servants, and emphasizing his fear by blasphemy, only to become the herald of Pentecost in ushering in the Christian church. See the Twelve who had fled in terror on the crucifixion day ever afterward ready to face men—that meant facing death itself. The receiving of comfort is the receiving of strength to help others. Bear witness, ye whose hearts have been torn with sorrows; only they who have known strength given in suffering can impart strength of comfort. The brilliant jurist, William Wirt, was made a Christian by one of his slaves; so in sorrows it is not the dignity of station, nor the degree of learning, nor the brilliancy of acquirements, but the suffering hearts that give us strength and hope.

A little incident in the life of Grisi, upon first meeting Jenny Lind, illustrates the power of the same heart for scorn or for comfort. It was in the presence of the royal household of Britain. By command of the queen each was to sing. The impulsive blood of the tropics was to be met by the favorite of the northern kingdom. Haughty with her brilliant triumphs, the Italian face of Grisi reflected her contempt of the gentle girl beside her. The proud daughter of Italy chilled the confiding heart of the "nightingale of Sweden." She had not learned the profound secret underlying the strength of character in the greatest of the prophets: "He must increase, but I must decrease."

The young singer took her place with trembling before the royal audience, only to shrink in fear before the scorn of the one who should have given courage. The accompanist had struck the opening chords, and in the breathless expectation all were surprised to see Jenny Lind turn and request him to rise. The music she was to sing she laid one side. Seating herself at the instrument with downcast gaze, she swept its keys with sweetest, gentlest touch. In another moment she breathed forth in song a simple prayer of her childhood. The Hearer of the singer was a greater than Victoria. The agony of the hour made her petition vocal with plaintive pleadings. As she lifted her face toward heights her prayer was reaching, the silence, except of her voice, seemed almost vocal with angelic notes. No strains like these had ever before been heard in the royal hall. She did not look upon Grisi or upon the queen and the royal family. She was the lonely girl of Sweden amid the royal pomp and splendor.

Not once did Grisi take her gaze from the young girl—not even to catch the absorbing fascination expressed by the queen. Upon the dark eyelashes of the Italian tears stood like pendent jewels. The flush on her cheeks had melted into radiant beauty. Her breath was choked back by inarticulate sobs.

When the singer had ceased her prayer no royal applause broke the silence. With an impulsiveness like her nature, with eyelashes suffused with weeping, with forgetfulness of courtly etiquette, Grisi hastened forward to draw the beautiful rival within her embrace, while she kissed the upturned lips. There was admiration in place of scorn, gentleness in place of pride. The same heart could scorn or comfort, hate or love.

The refusal to give comfort reveals our own base motives, while the desire to render help indicates a true character. God has made each of us a possible human comforter.

Comfort results from real excellence and strength. The men may be unknown who forge the anchor for the ship. Through heat and smoke and wearying din the work is carried on. No flaws are allowed to mar the workmanship. A single brush of paint might cover up any such defect; but the men are doing good work. What if a bubble were left in the welding—the owner of the ship could not detect it under the paint.

The huge contrivance is finally transferred from the foundry to the ship. There it rests, admired by crew and passengers voyage after voyage. Perhaps for months it is never wetted by the waters of the seas, except as they are sweeping the deck in heavy gales. The ship holds the monster fabric that was made to hold the ship. The men clean it of rust as though it were some showy thing, until the day of heaviest tempest comes. Against winds and mountain waves the trembling monarch of the ocean becomes a toy, as impotent as the tiny boats that childhood sails in glee. It is then the order is given to cast from its carriage the long-unused workmanship. In such a moment everything depends upon that single anchor. The terrific gale tautens the massive cable as though it were a thread in more than a giant's grasp. In vain the tempest shrieks through the cables of the ship as if they were strings of some Æolian harp builded by furies. The rolling mountain waves lash themselves into spray white as the shroud they threaten for the tossing ship. Faces of those longing for home are almost as colorless as the surfs outside. The captain's skill and courage are useless; he only watches in hope. It is the conflict of the anchor against the tempest and the sea; but the anchor holds. Had there been a flaw the splendid ship must have sunk to where the anchor held its mighty grip.

The anchor was the comfort of the ship. The comforters were the makers of that flawless anchor. The comforted were they whom the anchor saved. The anchor, like the ship, has become a thing of surpassing beauty. There is no comfort where there is not strength.

VII

INSPIRED TO INSPIRE

Useless man practically dead.—Self-denial for the sake of others the law of life.

First, world needs inspiring men.—Sheridan at Winchester.

Secondly, inspiration depends upon our ability to get away from self.—All conquest begins with conquest of self.

Value of each life is in the good done, not in the years lived.—Not size of the object that marks the power.

The weak have inspired the strong.—Children; invalids; sufferers.—Phillips inspired by his devoted invalid wife.

Thirdly, the world drops those who withhold help from others.—Memory takes care of those worth remembering. —Examples.

The inspiration we have measures how much we shall give.—Examples.

Two sources of inspiration: God and the immortal life.— Deniers of God and immortality cannot inspire others.

We grow toward what we believe.—They who live nearest God can lift others nearest him.

What we have learned in sorrows helps inspire others.— Chalmers.—Morrison.—The "Fresh-air Fund."

Discipline of life.—God needs inspired men.—Inspired lives and inspired writings.—Nothing right is secular.—Life worth living.

VII

INSPIRED TO INSPIRE

INSPIRATION is given to inspire. We give what we receive. We personify for others what we are ourselves. The man who is useless is practically dead, like water-soaked timber that will not burn and that builders will not use. In more senses than one "no man liveth to himself."

Nature in her abundance has nothing that exists for itself alone. Orchards grow to give fruit. Gardens bloom in exquisite beauty for the race. No one of least intelligence imagines that the sun shines for itself. Even the moon, dead and burned out, gives light. Were the ocean to leave its beaches dry, human life could not be sustained upon the globe. Fiercest storms are besoms to sweep the atmosphere; a land without storms of wind or rain would be a land of death. Vultures feeding upon carrion are scavengers of health. Insects are guardians against pestilence. Were our knowledge only broad enough we should observe that everything God has made is good. Each has its use. God is the great utilitarian.

It is not reasonable to assume that the finished work of God reverses this law. Is man exempt? Altruism is a term as recent as the French philosopher Comte; but its principle is as ancient as the race. Must we leave consolation of the suffering to voices of inanimate flowers? Can we, made in God's image, be dumb? Shall we leave the brightening and refreshing of the needy and deserving to the fruits that depend upon the dews and rains? Will God excuse our negligence of duty? Must all the sunshine in the chamber of pain come from the sun? Have we no light to shine? Must trembling hands be left to carry their own burdens? Is our strength not given to help the weary?

He whose hand was the first reddened with human blood attempted to evade the law by his interrogation, "Am I my brother's keeper?" The keen questioner of Christ felt the rebound of his own query when the Master reversed his words, "Who is my neighbor?" into the personal inquiry, "Am I neighborly?" Parable and direct teaching of the great Teacher, cumulative digests of apostolic advice, all declare the unmistakable necessity laid upon every one to be faithful to duty. Our light must shine. We must do good unto all men. We must bear others' burdens. We must go into all the world for Christ's sake. Self-denial for the sake of others is the law of Christ.

Notice, first, *inspiration as a factor in human well-being.* We use the term in its general sense, not theological. The world needs inspired men just as truly as it needs the inspired Book. Inspiration is not creation. It is the parent's duty to inspire; he does not create new powers in the child. It is the physician's duty to inspire his patient; he does not give strength, but helps the patient recover what was sinking lower and lower.

Children take their troubles to the mother for the inspiration she shall give. Pupils with hard problems go to the teacher, not to have him work out the problem, but to give them inspiration to work on. People in difficulties go to neighbors to get the same stimulating help. Sheridan at Winchester, riding his foam-swept horse, turned the retreating army into victors. He did not receive another recruit; the army was strong enough, but the hosts needed inspiration. The wife of Disraeli bore in silence the torturing pain from the careless driver's act of closing the carriage door upon her fingers, rather than depress the premier on his way to Parliament.

We may need inspiration ourselves one hour, and be called upon to give inspiration to others the next. The individual cannot tear himself away from the mutual obligations which make such helpfulness imperative.

Secondly, *this inspiration depends upon our ability to get away from self.* There is an infinite distance between the self-seeking man and the man of self-denial. The self-seeking man is ever suspicious that others will not give him what he imagines he deserves. He is sensitive lest his judgment shall be belittled. He who looks out for self first makes others' good an inferior matter. Real greatness begins as we get away from self and selfish desires.

Reason alike with Scripture emphasizes this fact. All true conquest begins with the conquest of one's self. Unless we school ourselves into obedience to what is right and true we cannot lead others into the truth. He who does not control himself cannot control others. All success begins with personal success. No one can be to others what he is not in himself first. He will not harm others until he has first harmed himself. Whatever our condition, this principle holds true.

No amount of labor or depression or sorrow can release us from duty. We cannot shut duty out by shutting ourselves away from it. Our obligations linger with our life.

Again, the value of our life is not in the years, but in the work done. "How old art thou?" is the least important question that can be asked. "What hast thou done?" is far greater. The finished life does not always tremble with the weight of the years. This Republic owes more to Hamilton than to almost any other man; and yet his work was finished at the age of forty-seven. Few lives have given greater power to the church than that of the scholarly missionary, Henry Martyn; but his earthly life was ended at thirty-one. The founder of modern missions in our churches, Samuel J. Mills, died at thirty-five. The consecrated name of Harriet Newell has done more in carrying out the last command of the Master to go into all the world with the gospel than many a veteran has done; and yet she died at the age of nineteen years.

Life is great or small according to what it has done. It is not the size of the object that marks the intrinsic power. If we could make a buttercup—just one—we could make the world. An infinite creative power—the same power—is necessarily back of each creation. The buttercup demands and declares the creative power as truly as does the swinging world. Life does not consist in doing one great thing, but in doing all things in the best way. Whether we do large things or small, the quality indicates what we are.

In other words, the truest life is not measured by the size or conspicuousness of the things done, but by the way of doing them. The life is in the doer, not in the thing. The cup of cold water will indicate many a great life in the final day. The visits to the sick or imprisoned will then unfold much of personal character.

We are not to fall back upon our lack of efficiency; we are simply to use what abilities we have at every opportunity. A grateful child is a perpetual inspiration to the father in his toils and cares. An invalid companion has been a constant loving inspiration to the one who spares no strength in his care for her. The ability to inspire others does not necessarily require great physical strength or health. The feeblest sufferer may enthuse the popular hero in his unremitting responsibilities. The name of Phillips has in it the luster of immortal fame; yet the inspiration because of which he faced mobs unappalled came largely from the suffering wife in his own home. Threats of burning the house over her head did not cause a moment's hesitation in her heroic consecration to the freedom of which her husband was the renowned advocate.

Thirdly, *the world drops from memory those who forget their kind.* People drop those who drop them. The world admires dignity, but responds to love. It salutes royalty in office, but is swayed by royalty of character. It does not put itself out for those who are bound up in themselves. It recognizes that the ruling factor in all society is love; and where love is, there is the constant doing for others. The real test is, not the magnificence of the house in which one lives, but how many homes one has made happier. There are such philanthropists in every community. Their overflowing sympathy is for those who suffer. They are always thinking of others.

Memory takes care of those worth remembering. The man who forgets others will drop out of memory with his burial. A good memory depends upon a useful life. The world gives its heart only to those whose hearts were broad and sympathetic. Good deeds inspire remembrance in return. Not how much one is to himself, but what he is to others, is the test. Not how much he gets for himself, but in what measure he shares his good things with others—this is the true worth of each. God has so fashioned us that the infirmities of the honorable dead slowly pass back into oblivion, while their excellences appear in increasing beauty. "Their works do follow them."

It is impossible to free ourselves from this obligation to help others to the fullest extent of our ability. God has written his purpose into our very natures. Reason agrees with revelation in confirming this law of our being. The total value of our life consists in what we shall have done for others. So universal is this obligation that the world drops out from its memory those who are comparatively useless to its progress.

Suppose the prophets of God had halted in their message; the wheels of progress would have gone back. Suppose Garrison had kept silence, fearing the mob raging around him more than he feared injustice; the liberation of a race would have been imperiled. Suppose Whittier had turned away from the slave to make his verses attractive to those whom slaves were serving; where would history be? What if the great reformers had abandoned their struggles for liberty; civilization would have been crushed under a relentless tyranny. The only lives worth the paper on which their names are written are of those who have spent their energies in self-sacrifice for others' good. Commonplace men—men who float with the tide of public opinion or of their own ease—are beginning to be forgotten with the going down of the earliest setting sun. They who live for self are dropped from memory when the undertaker has finished his work.

We are not to carry others' burdens that they can carry as well as ourselves. True helpfulness consists in giving comfort; and comfort means giving strength to those who are weary by inspiring them when they hesitate or fail.

Confronting such an obligation to helpfulness is our utter inability of ourselves. We can pity, but that will not help. We may show sympathy, but men need far more than sympathy. How is such power gained? We cannot inspire others above the inspiration we have ourselves received. The inspiration of Columbus in a measure inspired his men above even their superstitions. The absolute conviction of Cyrus W. Field inspired men to risk their wealth in a wire touching two continents and buried purposely in the ocean. Samuel Adams, catching a vision of liberty on the bloody field of Lexington, helped inspire a continent to achieve its freedom. The vision of Paul on the Damascus road never grew dim. In the vision he saw the coming triumph of a greater than Cæsar. He was to suffer untold sufferings, but the vision was above them. He was to be brought before kings, but the vision of the greater than Agrippa made him bold. He stood among peoples reeking with the vices of heathenism; but the heavenly vision inspired him to inspire them to a nobler life. His power lay not in his bodily presence—

that was weak. It was not in excellence of speech—men called that contemptible. His marvelous power in rousing cities, in forming churches, in fixing the attention of kings, lay in his obedience to the heavenly vision and the Christ of his faith. The source of inspiration is outside and above us.

The strange fascination of Napoleon lay in his power to enthuse his army with the glory of France. Nelson at Trafalgar led his fleet into the battle with the ringing reminder that England expected every man in that fleet to do his duty. The watchword of Wellington was "duty"—and duty means something higher than the man urging its claims.

The two sources of human power and inspiration are the convictions, God and the immortal life. The two belong together. They hold above us the greater Being and declare an unending life. Men complain of the injustice of this life; the assurance of the other declares the righting of the wrongs.

Sad hearts take up the every-day burdens; but the life to come does not subsist upon the conditions of this. Aching hearts sigh over the departed; but our loss is their gain. It is this conviction of God and immortality that comforts the poor who struggle for bread while the tables of the affluent are loaded with more than can be used. Shivering honest sufferers gaze wistfully upon furs whose warmth might save them from wasting hectic; but thoughts of the immortal life cheer them on while multitudes pass them by unnoticed. Take away from hope these two convictions and earth would become a bedlam.

They who deny God and immortality cannot inspire others. They may have brilliancy of intellect worthy better thoughts; their speech may be as coming from lips touched with the honey of Hymettus; they may be gifted with sympathy tinged with pity; yet so long as they know not God, and intimate that there is no life beyond this life, they cannot inspire the weary and the poor and the bereaved. Human nature can become a drudge; it can endure privations; it can enter homes darkened by death. But to inspire such as these requires more than mere human words from intellects that do not know, and guesses from hearts that do not believe.

We grow toward what we believe. We grow up or we grow down, according to the objects we follow. Egypt represented her deity by beasts, and has sunk back to them. Rome made her gods vacillating and coarse; and nothing in the range of her debasing belief could keep the mighty empire from sinking back into the dirt. One may dwarf himself into a pygmy when he ought to be a giant. If it were possible to keep one through full-grown manhood wrapped up in childish playthings, he might grow to a giant's stature, but he would always remain a travesty on human nature.

Thought expands when it sees other villages than the one in which it lives. Allegiance to the nation broadens us beyond that which comes from allegiance to the State. Plans laid involving other continents than the one oceans have bounded for our own broaden us yet more. The provincial has become a cosmopolitan with his knowledge.

Remember there are uncounted worlds among which this little earth is one. Remember there is another life somewhere. Let imagination wing itself to farthest possible outreach. The expanding vista broadens and deepens the mind and heart that takes it in. He who knows God and feels within his breast the throbbings of immortal life has something by which to inspire and stimulate others to a new purpose. The lever of Archimedes, by whose adjustment he promised to move the world, cannot compare with this power. They who live nearest God can lift others nearest to him.

Is it said we are too weak ourselves to help; we are too cast down to inspire; we are too broken-hearted to heal the breaking hearts of others? These are the very reasons why we can help and inspire others. Has God given you help? Tell others. Has comfort come to your dark hours? Tell others where it may be found for them. Has there come into your desolation the infinite compassion? Then stimulate others to find for themselves the same strength. If the believers of Christ would each begin with the first sufferer near them, and continue in such a work of inspiration for others, the world would take on a new appearance within less than twelve months.

The Christian world has not ceased to speak of Chalmers thrilling Scotland and Christendom from his Tron parish; pictures of his power are indelibly impressed upon the history of the influence of man upon men; yet who can tell us the name of the poor woman whose transcendent Christian life gave him week after week such inspiration? Yet this is history.

Narrators of what missions have done remind of Morrison's devotion to China: preaching the everlasting gospel, translating into the tongue of the empire the Word of God, laboring unceasingly with his two watchwords—the first, "It is my duty," the second, "Look up, look up;" yet who recalls the name of the faithful teacher in the ragged-school whose persistence won and inspired him to the life of usefulness that monumented her love?

Years ago a lady from the country visited a large city near her home. She was an invalid, and was touched by the sufferings of a little sick child whom she saw in the mother's arms in a filthy street. The thought came to her, "Why not take the child and its mother to my home?" She gave the invitation, which was gladly accepted. From the refreshing country life the weary mother and child went back well and strong. Some of the lady's neighbors, convinced of their privilege, followed her example. The next summer hundreds of children and their mothers were cared for in the same way; the following summer thousands more.

A neighbor of such a benefactor, poor and helpless herself, unable to care for even one, said she could at least give others the story of the charity. She wrote the account in a New York paper. The simple recital in the paper caught the attention of a lady of wealth, who sent her check for a thousand dollars to the editor, initiating the so-called "Fresh-air Fund." All over the United States, in England, and on the Continent, the work of caring for poor children has ever since that time been kept up. Had that invalid, as she passed the pale, sickly child, excused herself by saying she could not save all—"Why should I trouble myself with one?"—how much the world would have missed!

Inspiration is sympathy put into action. It makes the good of others our highest motive. It is Christ-like. Its method is to allow the divine will full power through us.

"Bear ye one another's burdens, and so fulfil the law of Christ." The inspiration and power imparted to each life must be divinely given. We cannot do our work well by leaving God out.

CONCLUSION.

In summing up the line of our thoughts we recognize the fact that self-denial is the cost of success. Self-discipline is the prerequisite to usefulness. We secure teachers who shall advise as to what we shall deny ourselves, and who shall administer discipline. Athletes and scholars agree in this method of preparation.

The burdens and deprivations of life are such conditions enforced. The denials and discipline we will not choose we are sometimes compelled to bear. Rightly used, they increase our power.

College life means a certain discipline, and the results tell. Life is a broader college, whose instruction makes larger, stronger men. Whatever God orders or permits leads to the same results. The true scholar is inspired by what he has learned; so in the larger life they who have profited by the severest lessons of divine ordering or permission are the most useful.

God needs inspired men and women. It is as needful that men shall be inspired to teach the inspired Book of God as it is to have the Book of God to teach.

The Bible itself is the best evidence that God inspires men other than those who were to make up the sacred writings. Who was the friend of God, the father of the faithful? And yet Abraham, thus distinguished, has not left us a single chapter. Take the whole history of Joseph, the incarnation of purity. To what scriptural character has there ever been given a diviner insight than to him? What life can we hold higher for a model? And yet this God-inspired man, this model for all ages, has not left a single line of his own writing upon either the shafts of Egypt or the pages of the sacred Word. Look at Jacob gaining such power with God that even his old deceitful nature became so changed as to require for him the better name of Israel; and yet even Israel never penned a line of Scripture. Where is there a single line written by that magnificent prophet of reform, Elijah? Where is there a Gospel according to Thomas? And yet he ranks first among the discoverers of the real nature of Christ.

Were not Abraham and Joseph and Israel in their living as truly inspired of God as was Moses, who recorded their history? Was a God-given inspiration lacking in Elijah, that example of greatest prophetic insight, while it was given to Samuel, who wrote his life? Was Thomas untouched by the Spirit of God when he broke forth in exclamation, "My Lord and my God"?

All through the Scriptures are the biographies of men who walked with God; their lives embalmed by other men commissioned as divine scribes. What is inspiration but being moved and animated by a supernatural influence, and that supernatural influence direct from God?

A special divine illumination is as much required for understanding the Word as was demanded in writing it. The doctrine of prayer is really an emphasis to an inspiration direct from God. The world is to be saved by inspired men. Bezaleel was as truly divinely chosen for his art as was Isaiah chosen to teach. God needs and demands inspired men to carry on his transcendent work in the saving and redeeming of the world.

Recall again among modern names that of Garrison, and the odds against him. The illustration will indicate the possible power in a strong, determined life. Two generations ago we were a slave nation. Our laws were in favor of the slave-driver. Our judges issued decrees against the slave. Our Northern free States, so called, were open for the sheriffs of slavery. The boast was openly made that the roll of a plantation's slaves would be called from Bunker Hill. Many churches were timid. Politicians were boldly on the side of the South. Merchants feared failure if agitation were kept up. Liberty was pinioned.

At such a time Garrison began his lifework. His was the consciousness of strength that comes from being right and doing a divine work. He stood alone, yet not alone. He was mightier than all the forces opposing him. His decision was greater than those of the supreme bench. Beside him Presidents were almost pygmies. While he worked on Congresses kept compromising. He was stronger than all the laws they made, and would snap these apart like hempen cords singed with fire.

He was a prophet indeed. He was doing God's work. He was inspired, and his inspiration inspired others until a nation gave him honor.

In God's sight nothing that tends to help others is secular. Every-day duties are divine, like larger obligations. To do well our work we must "be endued with power from on high." What is this but inspiration? We need the discipline of the schools. We imperatively require the divine help. We gain larger abilities by the severest discipline. We are inspired by suffering to make life easier for others. This possibility makes life worth living, even when days would otherwise be dark and the years desolate.

"NOT TO BE MINISTERED UNTO, BUT TO MINISTER."

Addresses, Sermons, and Essays.

Essential Christianity. By Rev. Hugh Price Hughes. 12mo, cloth,..$1.25

Fully sustains the reputation of this famous London preacher.

Ten Minute Sermons. By Rev. W. Robertson Nicoll, D.D. 12mo, cloth, gilt top.. 1.50

Brilliant sermonettes by the editor of "The Expositor's Bible."

Three Gates on a Side, and Other Sermons. By Rev. Charles H. Parkhurst. 12mo, cloth, gilt top.......................... 1.25

"Dr. Parkhurst is certainly a preacher of unusual power, and a thinker of marked originality."—*The Churchman.*

The Ideal of Humanity in the Old Times and New. By Prof. John Stuart Blackie, author of "On Self Culture." 12mo, cloth 1.00

"Fresh, forcible and practical. In close and helpful touch with everyday life."—*The Congregationalist.*

Sermons by the Rev. John McNeill. Vols. I., II. and III., each containing 26 Sermons. 12mo, cloth, each................ 1.50

"The Rev. John McNeill has a firm hold of Gospel truth, a clear mind, and a peculiar and graphic method of expressing sound convictions."—*Rev. John Hall, D.D.*

Twelve Sermons by the late Eugene Bersier, D.D., of l'Eglise de l'Etoile, Paris. Translated by Mrs. Alexander Waugh. With portrait. 12mo, cloth... 1.25

"We have read these sermons with very great delight. Bersier was a preacher of eloquence, force, and profit."—*The Independent.*

Princeton Sermons. Chiefly by Professors in Princeton Theological Seminary. 12mo, cloth............................... 1.50

The contributors are President Patten, and **Professors Green,** Hodge, Warfield, Aiken, Murray, and Davis.
"Scholarly, vigorous, and practical."—*The Congregationalist.*
"Coin from the royal mint of the King of Heaven."—*The N. Y. Observer.*

Pacific Coast Pulpit. Sermons by Representative Preachers on the Pacific Coast. With 17 portraits. 12mo, cloth.......... 2.00

Divine Balustrades, and other Sermons. By Rev. R. S. MacArthur, D.D. 12mo, cloth..................................... 1.25

"Marked by mental precision, and an atmosphere of spirituality that is decidedly refreshing."—*The Golden Rule.*

Sermons. By Rev. John A. Boardus, D.D. 12mo, cloth..... 1.00

Baccalaureate and Other Addresses. By Rev. E. A. Tanner, D.D., late President of Illinois College. 12mo, cloth....... 1.50

*** *See also Moody, Meyer, Herron, Stalker, and Spurgeon.*

The Life and Words of Christ.

The Public Life of Christ. Being a Chart of Christ's Journeys and a Map of Palestine, so combined as to present to the eye the mutual relations of the Chronology and Geography of the recorded events in the life of Christ, together with a harmony of the Gospels. By Rev. C. J. Kephart, A.M. Size, 24x36 inches. Pocket forms, cloth, 75c.; leather...................$1.00
Wall map form... 1.25

"Among the ingenious devices for the graphic description of our Lord's life and history we have seen nothing more effective."—*The Independent.*

Earthly Footprints of Our Risen Lord, Illumined. A Continuous Narrative of the Four Gospels according to the Revised Version, with introduction by Rev. John Hall, D.D. Illustrated by 113 full-page half-tone reproductions. *Third Edition.* Small 4to, cloth, net, $1.50; gilt edge with silk book mark, boxed, net, $2.00; full morocco, flexible, gilt edges, round corners, boxed ....net, 3.75

"To many the life of the Christ will be a new book in this form. Though beyond the introduction it contains no word except what is found in the four Gospels, yet when read continuously the narrative takes on new force and lifelikeness."—*The Golden Rule.*

The Life of Jesus Christ. By Rev. James Stalker, M.A. 12mo, cloth .... .60

A Critical Harmony of the Gospel (Christ in the Gospels). By James P. Cadman, A.M. Introduction by Rev. P. S. Henson, D.D. 8vo, cloth.. 1.50

"By its ingenious arrangement a close comparison between the narratives can be made with great facility."—*The Independent.*

A Harmony of the Four Gospels. With Explanatory Notes and References to Parallel and Illustrative Passages. In the words of the authorized version. By Edward Robinson, D.D. Edited by Benj. Davies, Ph.D. 16mo, flexible cloth............... .60

The Fifth Gospel. The Land where Jesus Lived. By Rev. J. M. P. Otts, LL.D. *Second Edition.* With 4 maps and many other illustrations. 12mo, cloth....................................... 1.25

"It claims to be just what it is, as series of sketches of certain events in our Lord's life and of certain localities which throw a special light on certain passages, brought up for review."—*The Independent.*

A History of the Preparation of the World for Christ. By Rev. David R. Breed, D.D. *A New and Revised Edition.* With illustrations. 8vo, cloth, gilt top....................... 2.00

The Christ. By Rev. James H. Brookes. 12mo, cloth...... 1.25

Notes on the Parables and Miracles of Our Lord. By R. C. Trench. Two volumes in one, large 8vo, cloth............. 2.00

The Problem of Jesus. By Rev. George Dana Boardman. 12mo, half-cloth... .35

Christian Evidences, etc.

Many Infallible Proofs. The Evidences of Christianity. By Rev. A. T. Pierson, D.D. 12mo, paper, net 35c.; cloth $1.00
"Only a man of wide and of broad sympathies, and one who had himself come up out of a conflict with doubts, could have so completely covered the whole battlefield of unbelief, meeting the doubter at every point with a candor that captivates, and a logic that conquers."—*The Morning Star.*

None Like It. A Plea for the Old Sword. By Rev. Joseph Parker, D.D., author of "The People's Bible." 12mo, cloth 1.25
A defense of the inspiration and authority of the Bible.
"The spirit of the work is as sweet as its blows are sturdy. This volume is one of the ablest on its side and is sound in its principles."—*The Congregationalist.*

I Believe in God the Father Almighty. By Rev. John Henry Barrows. D.D 16mo, cloth, gilt top........................ 1.00
"This is a bright and strong series of four addresses by a bright and strong man. They are rich in illustration, full of pith, and right to the point."—*The Independent.*

A Lawyer's Examination of the Bible. By H. H. Russell. 12mo, cloth... 1.00
"The case of the Bible is presented in such a way as to satisfy the demands of the intellect as well as the heart."—*The N. Y. Observer.*

Atonement: The Fundamental Fact of Christianity. By Rev. Newman Hall, D.D. 12mo. cloth......................... .75
"This valuable little volume will do much to assist in their study of this important subject those who may not have access to more elaborate works or leisure for the study of them. It is a book which cannot have too large a circulation."—*Christian Work.*

Unsettled Questions Touching the Foundations of Christianity. By J. M. P. Otts, D.D. 12mo, cloth....................... 1.00
"The author recognizes the fact that young men are sometimes harassed with doubts and questions, and he does his best to dispel the first and to answer the last. The simplicity and force of his reasoning will do all this for many inquiring minds."—*The N. Y. Observer.*

The Highest Critics vs. The Higher Critics. By Rev. L. W. Munhall, M.A. 12mo, cloth............................... 1.00
"The appearance of this volume is timely. The style is plain and pointed, and the argument critical and cumulative. We commend it to all."—*The Religious Telescope.*

The Evidences of Christianity. By William Paley, D.D. Edited by Canon Birks. Introduction, Notes, and Supplement. 12mo, cloth... 1.20

Ten Reasons Why I Believe the Bible is the Word of God. By Rev. R. A. Torrey. 16mo, paper............................ .15

⁎ *See also Brookes, By-Paths, and Living Papers.*

Devotional.

Prayers for Heart and Home. Morning and Evening Devotions for a Month. By Rev. F. B. Meyer, B. A. 8vo, flexible cloth .... $ .75

Daily Family Prayers for a Year. By Rev. J. R. Macduff, D.D. 4to, cloth... 1.50

A Guide to Family Devotion. Prayers, Scripture Readings, and Hymns, Morning and Evening, for a Year. By Rev. Alexander Fletcher, D.D. 4to, cloth................................. 3.00

A Gift of Love, and Loving Greetings for 365 Days. By Rose Porter. Long 18mo, cloth, $1.00; white cloth, silver top, boxed, $1.25; decorated silk, gilt edges, boxed................ 1.75

A Gift of Peace, and Loving Greetings for 365 Days. By Rose Porter. Long 18mo, cloth, $1.00; white cloth, silver top, boxed, $1.25; decorated silk, gilt edges, boxed................ 1.75

Daily Food for Daily Life. With border. Cloth, red edges, 15c.; white enamel covers, gilt edges....................... .40

Havergal's Complete Poems. 8vo, boxed.
  1. Cloth 2.00
  2. Cloth, full gilt.. 2.50
  4. French morocco, padded, gilt roll. red under gold edges, 4.00
  5. Persian calf, padded and embossed, gilt roll and red edges 5.00
  6. Three-quarter calf, gilt top, trimmed edges, gilt marbled paper sides.. 4.50

Prayers from the Poets. A compilation. By Martha Harger. 16mo, cloth, gilt top 1.00

The Gates of Praise, and other Original Poems. By Rev. J. R. Macduff, D.D. 18mo, cloth................................... .60

The Gates of Prayer. Private Devotion for Morning and Evening. By Rev. J. R. Macduff, D.D. 18mo, cloth............ .60

"My Guest Chamber;" or, For the Master's Use. By Sophia M. Nugent. 18mo, cloth, 50c.; white vellum cloth............. .75

Jesus Himself. By Rev. Andrew Murray. With portrait of the author. 18mo, cloth.. .50

Love Made Perfect. By Rev. Andrew Murray. With portrait of the author. 18mo, cloth.. .50

COMFORT AND CONSOLATION.

The Transfigured Valley. By Rev. William Miller. 16mo, cloth .... .50

Wells of Baca; or, Solaces of the Christian Mourner. By Rev. J. R. Macduff, D.D. 24mo, cloth, gilt top................. .50

The Life Beyond. An Allegory. By Mrs. A. Gatty. Adapted M. A. T. 32mo, white vellum cloth......................... .40

www.ingramcontent.com/pod-product-compliance
Lightning Source LLC
Chambersburg PA
CBHW031455160426
43195CB00010BB/981